Pub Walks
the
SOLENT WAY

*Walking titles by Countryside Books
covering the county of Hampshire include:*

Pub Strolls in Hampshire & the New Forest
Anne-Marie Edwards

Pocket Pub Walks in Hampshire
Nigel Vile

Pocket Pub Walks in the New Forest
Anne-Marie Edwards

Village Walks in Hampshire
Anne-Marie Edwards

Short Walks from Pubs in the New Forest
Anne-Marie Edwards

Hampshire & the New Forest Teashop Walks
Jean Patefield

Adventurous Pub Walks in Hampshire
& the New Forest
Nick Channer

The New Forest Companion
Anne-Marie Edwards

Pub Walks Along
the
SOLENT WAY

Anne-Marie Edwards

COUNTRYSIDE BOOKS
NEWBURY BERKSHIRE

First published 2002
© Anne-Marie Edwards 2002
Reprinted with revisions 2007

COUNTRYSIDE BOOKS
3 Catherine Road
Newbury, Berkshire

To view our complete range of books,
please visit us at
www.countrysidebooks.co.uk

ISBN 978 1 85306 738 9

Photographs by Mike Edwards

Typeset by CJWT Solutions, St Helens
Produced through MRM Associates Ltd., Reading
Printed by Borcombe SP Ltd., Romsey

Contents

Introduction 8

Walk

1   Christchurch and Stanpit Marsh:
(Solent Way: Christchurch – Mudeford Quay 4 miles)
Ye Olde George Inn (3½ miles) 11

2   The smugglers' coast – east of Barton on Sea:
*(Solent Way: Mudeford Quay – Barton on Sea –
Taddiford Gap 7 miles)*
The Beachcomber (5 miles) 17

3   Milford on Sea, Hurst Spit and Keyhaven:
*(Solent Way: Taddiford Gap – Milford on Sea –
Keyhaven 4½ or 5½ miles)*
The Smugglers' Inn (5½ or 6½ miles) 23

4   Wildlife magic – Pennington and Oxey Marshes:
*(Solent Way: Keyhaven – Moses Dock –
Lymington Town Quay 5½ miles)*
The Gun Inn (5 miles) 29

5   'By sea and forest enchanted' – Lymington
and Pylewell Park:
*(Solent Way: Lymington Town Quay –
Bucklers Hard 9 miles)*
The Ship Inn (7 miles) 35

6   A delight for all seasons – the Beaulieu river:
*(Solent Way: Bucklers Hard – Beaulieu –
Hythe Pier 9 miles)*
The Royal Oak (7½ miles) 41

7   By the Dark Water – a hidden New Forest valley:
*(Solent Way: Hythe Pier – Southampton –
Weston Point, Southampton Water 2 miles)*
The Bridge Tavern (4 miles) 47

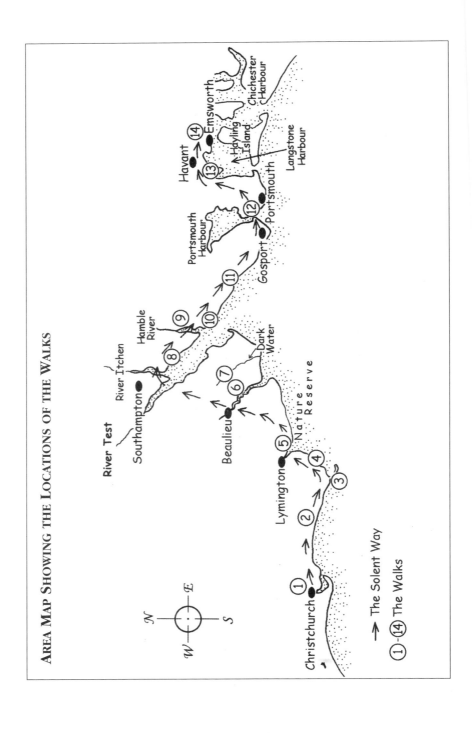

AREA MAP SHOWING THE LOCATIONS OF THE WALKS

→ The Solent Way

①-⑭ The Walks

Walk

8 Royal Victoria Country Park, Netley Abbey and the
Westwood:
*(Solent Way: Weston Point, Southampton Water –
Royal Victoria Country Park – Hamble Ferry 6 miles)*
The Prince Consort (4 miles)   53

9 Hamble and Bursledon – the 'Howards' Way' walk:
*(Solent Way: Hamble Ferry – Warsash
Landing, car park ½ mile)*
The Victory Inn (6½ miles)   59

10 Hook-with-Warsash Nature Reserve:
*(Solent Way: Warsash Landing, car park –
Brownwich valley 4 miles)*
The Rising Sun (4½ miles)   65

11 The Meon shore – Hill Head Harbour and
Titchfield Haven:
*(Solent Way: Brownwich valley – Hill Head –
Gosport Ferry 11 miles)*
The Osborne View (8½ miles)   71

12 Spice Island and Southsea Common:
*(Solent Way: Gosport Ferry – Historic Ships –
Old Portsmouth – Southsea Castle 2½ miles)*
The Wellington (4 miles)   77

13 World of the wild geese – Farlington Marshes:
*(Solent Way: Southsea Castle – Portsea Island –
Farlington Marshes, north-east 8 miles)*
The Compass Rose (4½ miles)   83

14 Harbour lights – Langstone and Emsworth:
*(Solent Way: Farlington Marshes, north-east –
Bedhampton – Langstone – Emsworth 6 miles)*
The Ship Inn (5 miles)   89

❧✿❧

INTRODUCTION

The Solent Way is a splendid walkers' route along the Hampshire coastline. This is a new illustrated edition of my guide to the Way, first published in 1994, containing fourteen circular walks along the Way and links giving details of the full linear route. This new edition includes the improvements which have been made recently to the Solent Way and all the walks have been revised and brought up to date. They provide safe family rambles between 3½ and 8½ miles in length and, apart from walk 7, each incorporates an interesting section of the Way. Perhaps the most welcome feature of this edition is that now every walk starts from a good pub where you can be sure of a warm welcome and excellent food and drink. I give some details of what food and drink are available, together with opening times and telephone numbers. (Opening times may be affected by the new regulations, and the beers on offer and the menus are frequently varied.)

As in the first edition, this book can also be used as a guide to the full 70 mile linear route of the Solent Way since each chapter contains special notes linking each section. At present the marked route runs from Milford on Sea, a few miles east of Christchurch, to Emsworth on the Sussex border. Future plans may include a westward extension so I have started these walks from Christchurch. I include a suggested linear coastal route to link Christchurch with Milford on Sea.

The section of the Solent Way included in each circular walk is indicated by the distinctive logo used on the signs marking the Way. The logo also indicates the start of the links if you are walking the full linear route. Every walk is accompanied by a sketch map based on notes made whilst checking out the route on the ground. They are designed to give an overall view of the route but for more detailed information arm yourself with the relevant Ordnance Survey Outdoor Leisure or Explorer map noted in the introduction to each chapter.

You will find your walk along the Way a unique experience. The creeks and harbours of Hampshire's coast have witnessed some of the greatest events in England's history and in spite of modern pressures most of the route is still beautiful and rich in wildlife. The scene is constantly changing. The bird-haunted marshes of Keyhaven and Pennington, the remote nature reserves around Warsash and Titchfield Haven, and the wide heaths and ancient woodlands of the New Forest form a striking contrast with the historic waterfronts of Southampton and Portsmouth and bustling riverside villages like Hamble, colourful with fishing boats and yachts.

This attractive coast has been settled since earliest times. Flint tools and axes have been found indicating that people may have been here before the last Ice Age when southern Britain was linked to the European continent and in the place of the Solent a great river ran from west to east. About 7,000 years ago sea levels rose, drowning the river and creating the coastline we recognise today. Subsequent waves of invaders have left tangible signs of their presence along the Way. The Romans were among the first to build sea walls and enclose areas of saltmarsh to make salt pans, initiating an industry that flourished between Keyhaven and Lymington until the middle of the 19th century. The salt pans remain, clearly visible as you walk the sea wall.

With the coming of the Normans, Southampton prospered as a leading commercial port. The sheltered waters of the Solent and Spithead made an ideal haven for the fleet and the Tudors began the construction of a great chain of castles and forts, including Hurst and Southsea, built to defend the Solent shore and to ring the main naval base, Portsmouth. Stones to build them were often taken from the churches and abbeys destroyed at the Dissolution of the Monasteries. Their ruins now grace the Way at Beaulieu, Netley and Titchfield. Villages like Bucklers Hard and Bursledon recall the days when the ships which formed England's 'wooden walls' were built on their slipways.

As you walk the Way you are rarely out of the sight and sound of the sea. The Solent, with its background of the Isle of Wight hills presents an everchanging picture of light and shade. There are still remote places where the only sounds you will hear are the murmuring of the waves on the beach and the cries of curlews over the marshes. No coastline can rival the Solent if you love the sea and ships. I wish you many magical hours walking its shores and exploring the surrounding countryside.

Anne-Marie Edwards

Acknowledgements

It is a pleasure to thank the following people for their help and encouragement:

Colin Piper, Hampshire County Council

The staff of Christchurch Tourist Information Office

The staff of Lymington Tourist Office

The staff of Havant Tourist Information Centre who introduced me to 'twittens'

The Westwood Rangers, Hampshire County Council, for information about Westwood Woodland Park and for the map drawn by John Bradman

Roy Underdown, Captain Dickie Snell and Andrew Blyth for information about Hamble and Warsash

Richard Sanders for information about Southsea Castle

Peter Holloway and Trish Furse for help with the Christchurch walks

Paul Eite who brought Langstone to life for us

My editor Paula Leigh and all at Countryside Books for their help and encouragement

Finally I thank my husband Mike for taking the photographs and being my companion on every step of the Way.

CHRISTCHURCH AND STANPIT MARSH

(Solent Way: Christchurch – Mudeford Quay)

Ye Olde George Inn

From the car park close to Christchurch's magnificent Priory Church this walk leads through the oldest part of the town to Stanpit Marsh Nature Reserve. The marsh is a surprisingly remote wildlife area of almost 150 acres. There are both salt and freshwater marshes, sandy banks, gravel beds and large stands of reeds providing the right conditions for a wide variety of birdlife and rare plants.

Christchurch, established by Saxon tribes on a ridge between the Avon and the Stour at the head of a beautiful almost land-locked harbour, still has the feel of a small Saxon town. Picturesque narrow streets link arms in front of its lovely Priory Church and standing high beside the mill stream are the ruins of a castle built by the Normans. Close by there is a rare example of 12th century domestic architecture, the Constable's House, added to the castle for the resident warden. Although roofless, the walls are almost intact and some of the window openings retain their delicate tracery.

Many charming old-world houses line the streets but one of the most fascinating must be Ye Olde George Inn. Here you will find a warm welcome and excellent food and drink. A former coaching inn where horses were changed on the long journey between London and Weymouth, the building dates back six hundred years. If the walls could speak what stories they would tell! Beneath its heavily beamed ceilings smugglers traded their contraband tobacco, brandy and gin probably brought from an underground tunnel leading up from the river. Hidden away in the roof is a priest's hideaway, and prisoners on their way to Poole docks for transportation were housed in the cellars. Princess Victoria, the future Queen, rested her carriage and horses in the spacious courtyard, now a pleasant place to eat in fine weather.

There are two comfortable dining areas where you can choose from a wide range of meals – try their honeyroasted ham, eggs and chips – and an interesting 'specials' board. We sampled a delicious chicken and leek pie. Real ales are Ringwood Fortyniner, Strong's Best, Boddingtons, Flowers Original and two guest ales. A good choice of wines is available and ciders are Thatchers and Scrumpy Jack.

The inn is open every day from 11 am to 11 pm, and food is served from 12 noon to 2.30 pm (3 pm at weekends) and from 6 pm to 9 pm. Telephone: 01202 479383.

- **HOW TO GET THERE:** Drive into the centre of Christchurch and follow the signs for Christchurch Quay. Turn right in front of the pedestrian precinct before the Priory, then after a few yards turn left to drive into the car park.
- **PARKING:** In the Priory car park.
- **LENGTH OF THE WALK:** 3½ miles. Map: OS Outdoor Leisure 22 New Forest (GR 160925).

THE WALK

1. Leave the car park by the entrance gates. The old house beside the gates was the porter's lodge, one of the few monastic buildings not destroyed during the dissolution of the monasteries in 1539. The Priory Church survived, claimed by the townspeople as their parish church. It dates from 1094 and among much that is beautiful is the splendid Norman nave flanked by semi-circular arches resting on

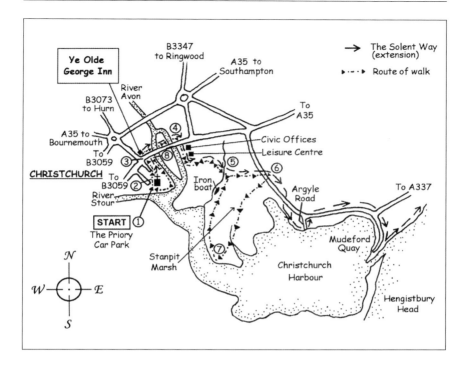

massive pillars, and the 14th century reredos behind the high altar which has told the Christmas story in carved stone to generations of worshippers who could not read.

2. Just past the porter's lodge turn right to walk diagonally left across the churchyard to go through iron gates into Church Street. Continue straight ahead to the corner of Castle Street. Ye Olde George Inn stands on the opposite corner.

3. Turn right along Castle Street to pass the half-timbered Old Court House and the ruins of the castle and cross the two bridges over the Avon.

4. After the second bridge, turn immediately right into Bridge Street car park. Keep straight on leaving the Civic Offices close on your left. (Ignore the footpath on your right.) Now walk diagonally left over the car park behind the offices, following the sign for the Leisure Centre. Keep straight on past the Centre along the side of the car park. A good

13

Town Bridge, a medieval five-arched bridge across the Avon

path leads you through a gate to walk beside a stream fringed with irises and kingcups. Keep to the path as it bears left to cross the stream.

5. Continue ahead across the recreation ground and take the right-hand path at a division to reach the car park adjoining the Stanpit–Mudeford road.

6. For the circular pub walk, you may now leave the Solent Way and turn right for a few yards then turn right again along the footpath to Stanpit Marsh. Soon a wide, very flat expanse of saltmarsh stretches before you, criss-crossed by narrow channels alive with birds. Herons poise like statues beside the water and golden and grey plovers peck at the mud with their short beaks. Looking west the marshes extend so far it seems you could walk dry-shod to Hengistbury Head! Just past the information hut you cross one of the slightly higher, sandy areas of the marsh. Here small pools bordered with mallows and meadowsweet attract colourful damsel and dragonflies in summer.

The path leads across a Bailey bridge over Mother Sillers Channel – named after a notorious 18th century smuggling family – and down to the harbour shore where it bears right beside Grimmery Bank. Now there is a wonderful view over the harbour especially southwards to the narrow entrance between Mudeford Quay and the sandbanks fronting the cliffs of Hengistbury Head.

7. Another right curve leads you beside the estuary of the Purewell stream to pass a wreck known as 'the iron boat'. Continue through a gate and bear left to rejoin our outbound route at Point 5. Bear left again and retrace your steps to the main road to recross the Avon bridges.

8. Immediately after the second bridge turn left to follow Convent Walk, a lovely path running between the swiftly flowing Avon and the mill stream. It curves round the Priory Gardens, giving good views of the Constable's House and the Priory. Turn right to cross the bridge, leaving another of Christchurch's historic buildings, Place Mill, on your right to return to the Priory car park.

 SOLENT WAY: Christchurch – Mudeford Quay (4 miles)

Although at present the officially designated Solent Way begins a few miles east of Christchurch at Milford on Sea there are plans to extend the route westward to Hengistbury Head. So I have anticipated the event with a suggested route eastwards from Christchurch. This is a noble journey along an historic coastline and it seems proper to start, as all great walks should, at a fine church.

From the Priory car park follow the route of the pub walk until you meet the Stanpit–Mudeford road at point 6. Turn right for a few yards, then leave the route of the pub walk (which turns right into the Stanpit Marsh entrance) and keep straight on beside the road towards Mudeford. After about 50 yards across a small green on the right a plaque marks the site of Tutton's Well. The water was said to be of 'uncommon purity' so it may possibly have given its name to the village of Purewell.

After about ¼ mile turn right following the footpath sign, then bear left along the harbour shore. This is a world of small boats, bobbing gently at anchor in the shallow water or pulled up on the shingle and piled with lobster pots.

The path leads to a slipway. Turn left here up Argyle Road to return to the main road and turn right to continue towards Mudeford. Cross the little Mude river and shortly afterwards you come to a narrow road on the right. Follow this to Mudeford Quay, which still has the aura of

The very charming Convent Walk

an old fishing port with its black and white cottages and old inn where tales are told of smuggling days. Between the quay and Hengistbury Head is the 'run' where the tide rips in and out of the narrow harbour entrance and rocks the fishing boats lying against the sea wall. In summer you can take a ferry across the entrance.

Now turn to Walk 2, page 21.

FACTFILE

To discover more about Christchurch's fascinating history visit the Red House Museum in Quay Street. Open Tuesday to Saturday from 10 am to 5 pm, Sunday 2 pm to 5 pm. Telephone: 01202 482860.

For a leaflet containing details of the wildlife on Stanpit Marsh and a map contact the excellent Information Office in the High Street. Telephone: 01202 471780.

THE SMUGGLERS' COAST – EAST OF BARTON ON SEA

(Solent Way: Mudeford Quay – Barton on Sea – Taddiford Gap)

The Beachcomber

❧

The Solent Way follows the coastline of Christchurch Bay to Milford on Sea and Hurst Spit. Although housing developments spread inland for part of the way there remains a delightful area where paths still lead over open countryside to the sea. During the 18th and 19th centuries smugglers landed their illicit cargoes at the coastal inlets known as 'bunnies' and led their laden ponies along these tracks. The circular route is a walk in their footsteps, taking you over Beckton Bunny and up Taddiford Gap.

Barton on Sea is a very old settlement, mentioned as being 'in the New Forest' in the Domesday Book. Axe heads dating from the Old Stone Age and Celtic pottery have been found on the Common. But very little of the old village remains. The soft clay of the cliffs, exposed to the full

17

force of waves whipped up by south-westerly gales, is being constantly eroded. But as the clay crumbles it reveals fossils known to be 45 million years old, the remains of sea creatures including crocodiles and sharks that flourished in the shallow seas which at that time flooded the chalk of the Hampshire basin. To discover more about the Barton cliffs, now a Site of Special Scientific Interest, you will find well-displayed information panels inside the Beachcomber café.

Although not a pub, the Beachcomber is licensed to serve drinks with meals and there is a well-chosen wine list. And there could be no better place to start your walk than the Beachcomber – one of my favourite haunts! Family-run, the atmosphere is warm and friendly. Everything is freshly cooked to order and includes a wide range of snacks – try their local sausages and home-cooked ham – as well as full meals. On our last visit we enjoyed a delicious liver and bacon casserole. Traditional oak-smoked kippers are a speciality. Sweets include Dorset apple cake.

In fine weather you can enjoy your meal in the clifftop garden. From the garden and the café there is a superb view over the western Solent to the Isle of Wight with the white stacks of the Needles sharply outlined against the sky.

The Beachcomber is open every day from 9 am, closing at 9.30 pm in summer and 6 pm in winter. Food is served all day. It is a good plan to reserve a table particularly at holiday weekends. Telephone: 01425 611599.

> • **HOW TO GET THERE:** Turn off the A337 for Barton on Sea and drive due south for about a mile to the sea front. Turn left in front of the obelisk to reach the Beachcomber which is almost immediately opposite.
> • **PARKING:** There is good roadside parking outside the Beachcomber, also two large public car parks close by.
> • **LENGTH OF THE WALK:** 5 miles. Map: OS Outdoor Leisure 22 New Forest (GR 239930).

THE WALK

1. Leave the Beachcomber entrance and turn right to follow the Solent Way over the wide green lawns fringing the cliffs on your right. When the houses on the left give way beside the golf course entrance keep straight on through two small gates and continue along the clifftop with the golf course on your left. In about ¾ mile the path dips to approach Beckton Bunny. Turn left to cross a bridge over this

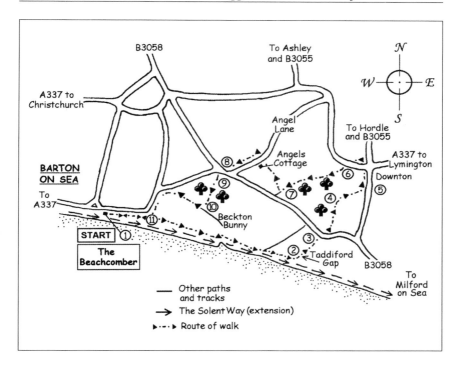

steep-sided inlet, then bear right to keep on along the clifftop. Pass a footpath sign on the left and continue for about ½ mile. The path dips towards the beach at the foot of Taddiford Gap, another bunny used by smugglers in times past. Now the inlet is almost choked by fallen cliffs and blocks of concrete which formed part of the coastal defences during the last war.

2. For the circular walk, leave the Way and turn left to follow the footpath up the shallow valley towards a distant line of woodland.

3. Cross a car park and go over the road, the B3058. A few yards to your right you will see a footpath sign indicating a field path on the left. Go through a gate and follow the path over the field with a deep ditch on your right. Cross a concrete bridge over the Danes Stream. According to Forest legend the Saxons once fought a fierce battle against the Danes nearby and every year on the anniversary of the battle the water turns red! Follow the path up a gentle slope into an oak wood and bear left along the edge of the trees.

Barton's crumbling cliffs reveal fossils over 45 million years old

4. Go through a gate and turn right across fields to meet a lane in Downton.

5. Turn left and follow the lane to the main road, the A337. Turn left past the pub and walk along the verge to a footpath sign on the left.

6. Bear left and follow the narrow path straight over a field to enter a wood. A beautiful path winds ahead through a jungle of ancient oak and ash trees. Their cracked and creviced branches provide food and homes for a wide variety of birds including treecreepers and woodpeckers. A rustic bridge leads over the Danes Stream once more, the path tunnels beneath arches of rhododendrons and climbs a little, and you emerge in a pine wood. Go over a crosstrack to leave the wood and approach the B3058.

7. Just before you come to the B3058 look carefully for a footpath sign on your right. Turn right and follow the direction of the sign over a field. Cross a stile and continue towards Angels Cottage. Go through a gate to the right of the cottage and turn left to follow Angel Lane to the B3058.

8. Bear right along the road for about 100 yards, then cross to a gravel track running beside the road on the left. Look carefully over the gravel for a footpath sign on your left, rather obscured by trees. (It is about 50 yards before a turning for Barton on Sea.)

9. Turn left to follow the sign through woodland then across more open land with the golf course on your left, towards the sea. Keep ahead ignoring all paths to left and right until you come to a narrow crosspath. (Just round the corner a metal gate leads to the golf course.)

10. At the crosspath turn right with a fence between you and the golf course on your left and follow an attractive path leading over the Common and through woods to meet a lane. Turn left to follow the lane to the clifftop.

11. Turn right to retrace your steps to the Beachcomber.

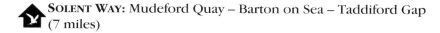 **Solent Way:** Mudeford Quay – Barton on Sea – Taddiford Gap (7 miles)

This is an interesting section of the Way with an opportunity to visit Highcliffe Castle and the attractive woodland at Steamer Point.

From Mudeford Quay turn left to follow the sea front promenade past the beach huts at Avon Beach. Continue past the next row of huts beneath Friars Cliff. The esplanade continues but a short detour will bring you to Steamer Point and Highcliffe Castle. Just after the last beach hut turn left up the cliff then bear half-right to follow the clifftop to Steamer Point Information and Display Centre beside the gates into the woodland, close to the Coastguard Training School. Leaving the Centre on your right follow the path through the woods. Just before you come to a house turn right and descend some steps to the beach.

Turn left and walk along the beach for about 200 yards, then climb the steps on the left to the car park at Highcliffe Castle. The Castle was built in 1835 for Lord Stuart de Rothesay who entertained many royal visitors there. The gardens were designed by 'Capability' Brown.

Return to the beach and head east for about a mile. At this point the Walkford Brook runs to the sea down Chewton Bunny, an attractively wooded valley. Turn left and take the footpath up the valley with the brook on your right. When the path ceases turn left up some steps to continue along a lane to the main road, the A337. Turn right beside the road as far as Western Avenue and turn right again to return to the clifftop.

Turn left to follow the clifftop to the Beachcomber. Follow the route of the pub walk as far as Taddiford Gap (point 1) and then turn to Walk 3, page 27.

FACTFILE

Wilts and Dorset buses run to Barton sea front from Lymington, Bournemouth and New Milton. Telephone: 01202 673555.

For details of the various activities taking place at Steamer Point contact the warden. Telephone: 01425 272479.

Highcliffe Castle is open daily for most of the year; from 11 am to 5 pm in summer, closing at 4 pm in winter. The gardens are open from 6.30 am to 6.30 pm in October to April; in May, August and September the gardens close at 9 pm and in June and July at 10 pm. Telephone: 01425 278807.

MILFORD ON SEA, HURST SPIT AND KEYHAVEN

(Solent Way: Taddiford Gap – Milford on Sea – Keyhaven)

The Smugglers' Inn

From Milford on Sea the walk follows the Solent Way, with a choice of two routes at the approach to Hurst Spit. You can either walk along the Spit to Hurst Castle and in summer take a ferry to Keyhaven, or reach Keyhaven by a shorter path along the edge of the marshes. Both routes are recognised as part of the Solent Way. At Keyhaven the circular walk leaves the Solent Way to discover a tiny village tucked away in a world of woods and streams. After passing Milford church and crossing the Danes Stream you return to Sea Road along a clifftop path.

Milford on Sea is a delightfully homely village. Cliff erosion gave Milford a sea front in the late 18th century and in spite of the attempts of a local landlord, Colonel William Cornwallis-West, to turn this former inland parish into a grand seaside resort, Milford retained its quiet dignity and old-world charm. The centre of the village is a pleasing mix of small shops, old inns and colour-washed cottages. The small village green is overlooked by the tower of a Norman church which has unusual lean-tos. Tradition has it that the window in the south lean-to was formerly used to smuggle beer for the bellringers!

Some smuggled beer no doubt found its way to the pub I have chosen for the starting point of this walk, the aptly named Smugglers' Inn. Built in 1803, this former coaching inn offers a warm-hearted welcome, excellent ales and tempting home-cooked food. There are two spacious bars with well-arranged eating areas and in cool weather there are blazing log fires in both. The older part of the inn with its low beamed ceilings is the haunt of the pub ghost. Only his leg has been visible up till now, briefly glimpsed as he disappeared through the wall! Real ales are Pride of Romsey, London Pride, Tetley's and a guest ale. Ciders are Strongbow and Scrumpy Jack and there is a well-chosen wine list. The menu is extensive and varied. Lighter meals include 'Smuggler's Lunch' – jumbo sausage, cheese and salad, and 'Fisherman's Lunch' – a pint of juicy shell-on prawns with a seafood dip. Main meals include a daily roast, and a choice of 'specials' which when we were there included chicken breast with lemon and apricot and mussels in white wine, garlic and cream sauce.

The pub is family-friendly with a real boat – ideal for budding pirates and smugglers – in the garden. Drinks and food are served all day from 10.30 am to 11 pm (Sunday 12 noon to 10.30 pm). Book ahead for Sunday lunch. Telephone: 01590 644414.

- **HOW TO GET THERE:** Approach Milford along the A337. In Everton head south along the B3058. In a little over a mile turn sharp left following the sign for Keyhaven. Cross straight over Milford High Street into Sea Road passing the Smugglers' Inn on your left and after a few yards turn left into the public car park.
- **PARKING:** In the public car park off Sea Road, close to the pub.
- **LENGTH OF THE WALK:** 5½ or 6½ miles. Map: OS Outdoor Leisure 22 New Forest (GR 292918).

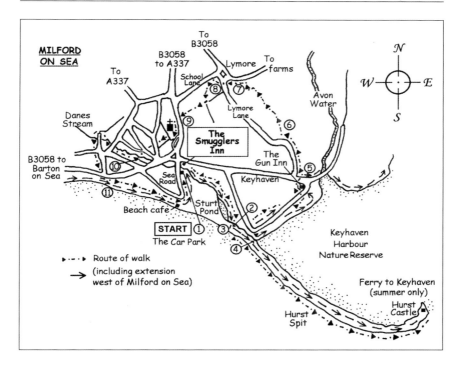

THE WALK

1. From the car park follow the footpath running east along the south bank of the Danes Stream, indicated by a Solent Way signpost. Cross a small bridge and continue to a road. Keep ahead, and when the road curves left continue along a gravel track. Bear right down some steps then follow the path with thick reed beds on your right. The reeds thin around Sturt Pond, a small lagoon thronged with birds especially in winter.

2. Cross the bridge at the point where the Danes Stream flows out of the lagoon and climb the shingle bank ahead to enjoy a wonderful view across the Solent to the Island and over Hurst Spit to the castle.

3. Bear left along the shingle bank with the Danes Stream running parallel on your left. When you come to another bridge on your left you can either follow the Spit to Hurst Castle (continuing to Keyhaven (point 5) by ferry in the summer months, or returning along the shingle to continue the walk from point 4) or take the shorter option.

25

4. To continue the shorter walk bear left, cross the bridge and follow the road to a joining track on the right. Take this track along the sea wall across the marshes. Pass a path on the left and continue along the sea wall to Keyhaven Harbour, the jetty and the ferry landing. Follow the road as it bears left in front of Keyhaven Yacht Club, then right past the Gun Inn.

5. Leave the Solent Way and keep straight on beside the road to a large grassy triangle and war memorial. Bear right before the grass to Lymore Lane and follow the lane as it curves left past the track to Vidle Van Farm.

6. Shortly after, turn right following the footpath sign for Lymore. The path doglegs left then right between fences. After a second dogleg, cross a stile and keep ahead beside a field with a hedge on the left to go over the next stile to a narrow lane in Lymore village.

7. Turn left along the lane as it winds past attractive houses half-hidden among copses of tangled willows and oak trees. Take the first lane on the left to rejoin Lymore Lane. Bear right, then turn almost immediately left into School Lane.

8. After a few yards turn left following the footpath sign for Milford. This leads through woods, then bears a little right beside a field with the woods on your right. When the woods cease bear left past a post supporting power lines and keep ahead to a prominent signpost. Turn right following the sign for Milford church to cross fields to the main road, the B3058.

9. Turn left along the pavement. Just before a road on the right leads to the church look for a small white gate on the right leading into the churchyard. Cross the churchyard and turn right to walk round the church tower (tower on your right) past a path on your left to a crossing path by a lamp standard. Turn left to leave the churchyard through a white kissing gate and keep ahead down the appropriately named Love Lane. Cross a road and continue along the lane to the next crossing road. Here, turn right for a few yards, then turn left down a footpath leading steeply downhill. Cross a small bridge, pass a track on your right and with the mill pond on your right continue to cross a bridge over the Danes Stream.

Sturt Pond with Hurst shingle bank in the distance

10. Walk up to a crosspath and turn right along the wooded valley with the Danes Stream on your right. Cross a road and continue with the stream still on your right. Go over a footbridge and continue with the stream now flowing on your left. When you come to a crosspath bear left, then left again to go over another bridge to Woodland Way. Follow Woodland Way towards the coast, cross a road then take De La Warr Road to the clifftop.

11. Cross the road and bear left along the clifftop towards Milford. At the Beach Café turn left to cross the road and walk up Sea Road to the car park.

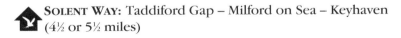 **SOLENT WAY:** Taddiford Gap – Milford on Sea – Keyhaven (4½ or 5½ miles)

This short section of the Way presents an ideal opportunity to visit Hurst Castle and enjoy the ferry ride to Keyhaven. You will be rewarded by marvellous views west over Christchurch Bay and east over Keyhaven Marshes, one of the finest bird sanctuaries on the south coast.

From Taddiford Gap climb Hordle Cliff and follow the path ahead towards Milford on Sea. These high cliffs, once used by smugglers as look-outs, made excellent vantage points during the Second World War and are still littered with the remains of gun emplacements.

Ahead you will see Hurst Spit and Milford. The path becomes gravelled as you approach the village and the cliffs slope gently down towards a large white building on the sea front. Leave the building on your left and when you reach the Beach Café, turn left to cross the road and walk up Sea Road to the car park. Follow the route of Walk 3 (taking either option) as far as the Gun Inn in Keyhaven (point 4) then turn to Walk 4, page 33.

FACTFILE

Wilts and Dorset buses serve Milford from Bournemouth, Christchurch and Lymington. Telephone: 01202 673555.

Hurst Castle is open from April to September, daily 10 am to 6 pm; weekends only from October to March. Telephone: 01590 642344.

The Keyhaven–Hurst Castle Ferry operates daily from April to the end of October. Ferries depart Keyhaven on the hour from 10 am and return from Hurst Castle on the half-hour until 5.30 pm. Some additional services. Telephone: 01590 642500.

WILDLIFE MAGIC – PENNINGTON AND OXEY MARSHES

(Solent Way: Keyhaven – Moses Dock – Lymington Town Quay)

The Gun Inn

The marshland between Keyhaven and Lymington is a spectacular wildlife reserve. The best way to explore this remote area is to follow the sea wall. This is the route of the Solent Way and forms the first 3 miles of the circular walk after crossing Avon Water. Among the birds you may expect to see probing the mud and saltmarsh for worms and shellfish – curlews, dunlins, redshanks and oyster-catchers – you may glimpse a rarity such as an avocet recognisable by its pencil-thin upturned beak. The production of sea salt was an important local industry until the early 19th century and you can still see signs of the former salterns. We return by field paths with a final look at the reed beds alongside Avon Water.

Keyhaven is an attractive little harbour dotted with fishing boats and the sailing craft of the Keyhaven Yacht Club and the Hurst Castle Sailing Club. They thread their way along the narrow channels through the marshes known as 'lakes'. One of the lakes is named after Colonel Peter Hawker, a noted 19th century wildfowler who owned a house in the village which he called his 'little gunning place'. He kept a diary for over 50 years and although his account of his exploits is somewhat bloodthirsty, his journals are an invaluable wildlife record.

Next to Colonel Hawker's house, opposite the large car park where we begin our walk, stands the appropriately named Gun Inn. The Gun is an early 17th century black and white pub with a slate roof and cottage-like sash windows. The porchway is surmounted by a small cannon and the walls are attractively draped with fishing nets and lobster pots. Inside there is a comfortable bar area, a family room and a cosy beamed 'snug'. Among the bar snacks are ploughman's lunches and a range of fresh salad platters which include local dressed crab. Cottage cheese and mixed fruit provides a light choice. Main courses include supreme of salmon coated with a hollandaise sauce and Cajun butterfly chicken breast.

Real ales are Wadworth 6X, Flowers Original, Marston's Pedigree, Strong's Best Bitter and Ringwood Old Thumper. The wine list includes some refreshing country wines and there is a choice of 130 malt whiskeys.

The garden, where you can enjoy barbecues in summer, has a play area for children. Opening times are from 11 am to 3 pm and 6 pm to 11 pm on Monday to Saturday. On Sunday the pub opens from 12 noon to 3 pm and from 6 pm to 10.30 pm. Meals are served from 12 noon to 2.20 pm and from 6 pm to 9.20 pm. Telephone: 01590 642391.

- **HOW TO GET THERE:** Follow the signs for Keyhaven from Milford on Sea. In Keyhaven the road turns right to the Gun on your right and the car park on your left.
- **PARKING:** In the large public car park opposite the Gun.
- **LENGTH OF THE WALK:** 5 miles. Map: OS Outdoor Leisure 22 New Forest (GR 305915).

THE WALK

1. With the Gun Inn on your left follow the lane immediately on your right. Harbour sights and sounds greet you as you cross the sluice gates over Avon Water. Boats rock gently in Keyhaven Harbour

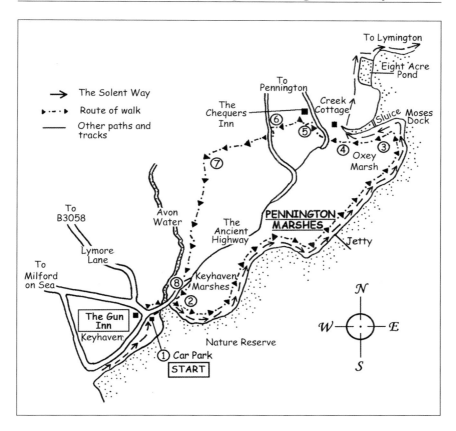

Legend:

→ The Solent Way

▶ ·· ▶ Route of walk

—— Other paths and tracks

To Lymington

Eight Acre Pond

To Pennington

Creek Cottage

Moses Dock

Sluice

The Chequers Inn

⑥

⑤

④

③

Oxey Marsh

⑦

To B3058

Avon Water

The Ancient Highway

PENNINGTON MARSHES

Jetty

Lymore Lane

To Milford on Sea

⑧ Keyhaven Marshes

②

The Gun Inn

Keyhaven

Nature Reserve

① Car Park

START

N
W — E
S

beside a jetty piled with nets and lobster pots. Gulls screech overhead and busy little turnstones scamper along the water's edge, tipping the pebbles over in their search for food.

2. Turn right following the Solent Way sign through a gate to walk along the sea wall. At low tide a vast expanse of marshland colonised by salt-resistant plants such as glasswort and cordgrass is revealed forming a paradise for huge numbers of birds. Much of the rough grassland north of the wall has been reclaimed for farming purposes but the embankments of the former salterns are clearly visible and also the mounds that once supported windpumps employed to force the concentrated brine into coal-fed boiling houses.

The sea wall skirts a pool on the left, a favourite playground for the rare little tern. This small bird is a delight to watch as it hovers over the

Keyhaven Harbour, looking towards the Isle of Wight

water, slender wings arching above its snowy back, before diving to catch a tiny fish in its black-tipped yellow beak. Follow the sea wall as it curves around the shore of Keyhaven and Pennington Marshes for over 2 miles. Ignore all footpaths leading from the wall on your left.

The sea wall now skirts Oxey Marsh. On your left you come to a small grassy promontory with a semi-circle of large flat stones. Formerly there was an inlet here and the stones are all that remain of 14th century Oxey Dock where coal barges once unloaded their cargoes. Continue along the sea wall which turns north along the left bank of an inlet, the entrance to Moses Dock, another former unloading depot for barges. On your right you come to a sluice gate.

3. Continue along the Solent Way, keeping straight on down some steps to pass the sluice gate on your right and continue with the inlet on your right. Turn right over a stile. Soon you will see Creek Cottage at the head of the old dock. One of the two Tudor barns close by was possibly a boiling house and the other was probably used for storing the salt.

4. Continue to a stile in front of Creek Cottage. For the circular walk, leave the Solent Way and turn left before the stile. Follow the path to a minor road. Bear right to follow the road past Chequers Green with the Chequers Inn just beyond. This old inn derives its name from 'Exchequer' as it was the house where the saltworkers' wages were kept. It is said that the inn is partly constructed from the timbers of a French fishing boat *Le Hareng Rouge*. Evidently its greedy crew overloaded the boat with winkles and it sank, much to the delight of the local fishermen!

5. Turn left following the footpath sign beside the Green. Cross a stile to take a very narrow footpath which leads over another stile into a meadow. Continue for just a few yards then turn right over a stile and then bear left again to resume your westward heading over fields and stiles to a lane.

6. Turn left along the lane for about 100 yards then turn right along a narrow tarmac path. The path curves right past a gate and becomes a grassy way bearing left to continue leading west. Cross a lane leading to a tip on the left, climb the stile ahead and bear left following the footpath sign.

7. A pleasant track now leads south with the Isle of Wight hills on the horizon. Keep to the main track as it doglegs right and left to continue south past a footpath on the left.

8. Go through a gate to join the Ancient Highway, a narrow road that used to link Lower Pennington and Keyhaven. Bear right at the side of the thick reed beds which almost conceal Avon Water. Swallows roost here and shy reed buntings may be glimpsed feeding on the seeds of the marsh plants. Retrace your steps over the sluice gates to return to the car park and Gun Inn.

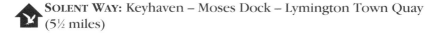 **Solent Way:** Keyhaven – Moses Dock – Lymington Town Quay (5½ miles)

Splendid views over the Normandy Farm Nature Reserve at the mouth of the Lymington river can be enjoyed as the Way continues along the sea wall and skins the former salterns beside Eight Acre Pond. A riverside walk past a forest of masts leads to Lymington Quay.

Follow the route of Walk 4 as far as the stile in front of Creek Cottage (beginning of point 4). Cross the stile and turn right along the gravel path running in front of the cottage and keep straight on passing the Tudor barns on your right. Keep ahead along a tree-shaded path to the 'Salterns'. During the Second World War this was the home of Commander Peter Ouvry, the first person to dismantle a magnetic mine so enabling the Allies to find a defence against it. Keep ahead to skirt Eight Acre Pond on your right. The route turns right to follow the coast towards a marina. Go through a gate at the approach to the marina and follow the sea wall to a small dock. Turn left for a few yards, then turn right to a footpath sign. Bear right past the marina office which is on your right to return to the sea wall and continue towards the quay.

After passing Lymington's fine sea water swimming pool established in 1833, the Way runs beside the sea wall past a park, then turns inland to take Quay Road. On the right is the Berthon Boat Co. named after the Revd Lyon Berthon, the designer of the famous collapsible lifeboat. The black and white house projecting into the road is called, appropriately, Pressgang Cottage. Formerly the Harlequin Inn, it was the headquarters of the pressgang in 1800. The road leads to the quay, overlooked by the Ship Inn. Now turn to Walk 5, page 39.

Now turn to Walk 5, page 39.

FACTFILE

There is no public transport to Keyhaven but Milford on Sea is only a mile away and can be reached by a pleasant walk along the sea front. For details of buses and ferries see Walk 3.

'BY SEA AND FOREST ENCHANTED' – LYMINGTON AND PYLEWELL PARK

(Solent Way: Lymington Town Quay – Bucklers Hard)

The Ship Inn

The phrase 'by sea and forest enchanted', sometimes used to describe the historic port of Lymington, could not be more appropriate. For centuries the town has been associated with the sea and shipping and north of the town lies the medieval landscape of the New Forest. From Lymington we cross Pylewell Park Estate then leave the Solent Way to take a beautiful path through Sowley Brooms, an ancient oak wood. Quiet lanes lead us back to Lymington Quay.

Until the end of the 18th century Lymington flourished as a port noted for its foreign trade, its salterns and the proceeds of what Daniel Defoe termed 'rogueing and smuggling'. Ships of up to 500 tons could berth by the town's cobbled quayside. These prosperous days came to a sudden end when in 1731 a Merchant Navy captain, William Cross, built his Toll Bridge Dam across the river. But today Lymington once again bustles with life. A commercial fishing fleet operates out of the quay, two large marinas and river moorings attract yachts from around the world and a regular ferry service runs to Yarmouth on the Isle of Wight.

On the waterside, overlooking this busy scene, stands the Ship Inn. This is a spacious and comfortable pub with a hearty welcoming atmosphere. Although the pub has a Victorian feel with its plush seating and windows decorated with coloured glass, the building is much older. Formerly it was a row of fishermen's cottages and I am told that tunnels, used to smuggle contraband, run from beneath the pub up the High Street to the Angel Inn.

A huge choice of meals is available. Among the snacks are baguettes with a variety of fillings and more substantial meals have the hungry walker in mind, offering for example, among many satisfying dishes, beef stew and dumplings. Sweets include a 'Back to Schooldays' menu – spotted dick and jam roly-poly! Real ales are 6X and Flowers IPA. Ciders and wines are also on offer.

The Ship is open from 11 am to 11 pm, (12 noon to 10.30 pm on Sundays) and food is served all day.

Telephone: 01590 676903.

• HOW TO GET THERE: Approaching from the north or west follow the signs for the town centre and the High Street. Drive down St Thomas' Street for about 50 yards then turn right for the car park down an entry just past Waitrose. Approaching from the east drive up the High Street, pass the church on your right and turn left following the car park sign. Avoid the crowds on Saturday, market day.

• PARKING: In the public car park off St Thomas' Street.

• LENGTH OF THE WALK: 7 miles. Map: OS Outdoor Leisure 22 New Forest (GR 321953).

THE WALK

1. From the car park return to St Thomas' Street. Turn right to pass the church on your left and walk down the High Street, a delightful mix of elegant Georgian houses, bow-fronted cottages and little courts and alleyways. Cross the road at the foot of the High Street and continue down cobbled Quay Hill which bears right to the quay and the Ship Inn.

2. Retrace your steps for a few yards to the foot of Quay Hill and follow the Solent Way signs along a lane. Turn left to follow Mill Lane and Waterloo Road past the station. Turn right over the level crossing and cross the Toll Bridge Dam.

3. Turn right and follow the waterside. The metal rails on your right cease and, opposite, two gravel tracks lead left from the road. Turn left, take the right-hand track and turn almost immediately left into the wood following the footpath sign. Walk uphill to the monument raised in memory of Admiral Sir Harry Burrard Neale who retained his crew's loyalty during the Nore mutiny.

4. Turn right down the lane beyond the monument, then take the first gravel track on your left past Halyards. Go through a gate and follow the path beside fields and through woods to a lane. Turn left for a few yards then turn right past Snooks Farm to a lane.

5. Bear right and cross straight over a minor road. Walk down the lane ahead, Shotts Lane, for about ¼ mile, then turn left along a wide track with fields on the right. Cross a track, keep ahead for a few yards then turn right to continue with a fence on your right. Over a stile the path leads beneath fine chestnut trees and pines before curving left still with the fence on your right. The mansion beyond the fence is Pylewell House. In 1875 the Pylewell Estate passed to William Ingham Whitaker. His grandson of the same name died a bachelor in 1988 and was succeeded by his nephew, the twentieth Baron Teynham.

Cross a stile and keep ahead through a small iron gate to go over a track. Go through an identical gate to follow a narrow path with a fence on the right. Keep to this narrow path to the left of a broader track along an avenue of pollarded limes past Dod's Pond. This was once the centre of South Baddesley village, destroyed in 1818 to create parkland. Follow the path ahead through a gate and across a stream. Continue beside a meadow and over a wooden footbridge to cross another field and stile to a track leading to a minor road.

6. Keep ahead along the road. Cross a cattle grid to the right of a grassy triangle and follow the footpath sign over a stile into a field. A lovely path leads beside fields then through the trees of Sowley Brooms.

7. When you come to a crosstrack the circular walk leaves the Solent

Way and turns left. When the path curves right, cross the stile ahead and bear a little left to cross another stile. Walk over a field and go through a gate to a lane.

8. Bear right, follow the lane up to a road junction and turn left for Norleywood village. Continue for about ¾ mile keeping straight on past a single track road on the right and shortly after another joining track on the right. When the lane begins to swing right turn left over a footbridge and follow a lane towards South Baddesley. You pass the little Victorian church of St Mary the Virgin, well worth a visit. Note the enormous pine tree in the grounds!

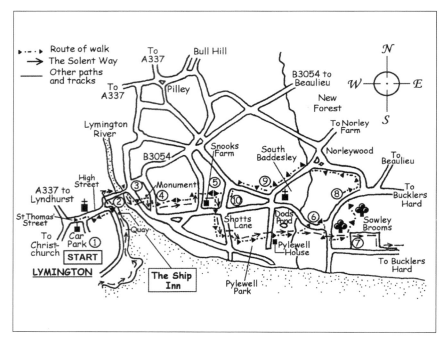

9. Take the first lane on the right which winds through oak woods and meadows for about ¾ mile to a lane on the left opposite a brick-walled drive entrance. Turn sharp left along the lane and after about 200 yards you will see a plaque on the right in front of a metal barn. This is close to one of the blister hangars of the wartime airfield constructed in this area in 1943 and commemorates the part played by American Thunderbolts during the D-Day landings. A little further down the lane

A blister hangar remains on the site of Lymington's wartime airfield, constructed in 1943

you meet the track on the right which we followed outbound at point 5.

10. Turn right to retrace your steps along the Solent Way past the monument to Lymington Quay. Walk up the High Street to your car.

 SOLENT WAY: Lymington Town Quay – Bucklers Hard (9 miles)

Although part of this section of the Way follows lanes they are mostly grass-bordered and cross countryside once farmed by Cistercian monks from Beaulieu Abbey. You will be reminded of them as you pass Sowley Pond created to satisfy their need for fish, the grange built for lay brothers at St Leonards and the ruins of their chapel.

From Lymington Quay follow Walk 5 as far as the crosstrack in Sowley Brooms in point 7. Do not turn left but keep straight ahead beside a field. Turn right at the next hedge with the hedge on your right, then turn left along the edge of the field. Go through a small wooden gate to

The Lymington river

the lane and turn left to follow the lane past Sowley Pond. Continue for about 1 mile to a T-junction and turn right. The lane leads past the grange at St Leonards and the ruined chapel still preserving a little delicate tracery within a window arch.

Shortly after St Leonards, the Way turns right then bears left along a narrow lane for about ¼ mile to Bucklers Hard. Cross a stile and walk through the village to the river. Now turn to Walk 6, page 45.

FACTFILE

Lymington is served by Wilts and Dorset buses from Southampton, Bournemouth and Christchurch. Telephone: 01202 673555. Also trains, telephone: 08457 484950.

For all information about Lymington contact the excellent Information Centre. Telephone: 01590 689000.

A DELIGHT FOR ALL SEASONS – THE BEAULIEU RIVER

(Solent Way: Bucklers Hard – Beaulieu – Hythe Pier)

The Royal Oak

*T*his walk connects two of the most fascinating villages in the New Forest – Beaulieu, the 'beautiful place' beside the river where Cistercian monks founded a great abbey in 1204, and Bucklers Hard, a perfectly preserved 18th century village where many of the ships for Nelson's navy were built. The riverside woods and fields formed the backdrop for the film 'A Man for all Seasons'. Even today, although yachts throng the river, shelduck families glide among the inlets and terns perfom their flying displays overhead. On quiet summer evenings nightingales still sing in the Beaulieu woods.*

A mile north-east of Beaulieu village the road to Dibden Purlieu runs up to Hilltop with roads leading off to Fawley and Exbury. Many coaches must have rattled over this busy junction in the past and many weary travellers found rest and refreshment at the charming old world pub where we begin this walk, the Royal Oak. This is a genuine New Forest pub with low beamed ceilings, comfortable seating and the friendliest of welcomes. Wooden panels depicting the various brand marks used by the Commoners to distinguish their livestock provide a link with Forest life. And from a wall chart you can discover how some well-known beers came to have such extraordinary names! Real ales are Morland Old Speckled Hen, Abbot Ale, Ringwood Best and Flowers Original. Interesting wines from around the world are listed including a dry white from the local Beaulieu vineyard. A wide range of snacks – salads, ploughman's lunches, filled baps – is available. Roasts and pies are popular main meals and among the 'specials' on our visit was a tempting breast of chicken cooked in tarragon and cider.

There is a large patio and a safe enclosed garden. Opening hours are from 11 am (12 noon on Sundays) to 3.30 pm and from 6 pm to 11 pm (10.30 pm on Sundays). Food is served from 11.30 am to 2.30 pm and 6 pm to 9.30 pm on Monday to Saturday and from 12 noon to 2.30 pm and 7 pm to 9 pm on Sunday. Telephone: 01590 612228.

• **HOW TO GET THERE:** The best approach is via the A326. Turn in the direction of Beaulieu along the B3054 and continue for about 2 miles to the pub at Hilltop.
• **PARKING:** Patrons may leave cars in the Royal Oak car park but it is wise to have a word with the management first.
• **LENGTH OF THE WALK:** 7½ miles. Map: OS Outdoor Leisure 22 New Forest (GR 401032) .

THE WALK

1. Leave the pub by the front entrance, cross the grass and turn left down the road towards Beaulieu (westwards along the Solent Way). Continue down the hill for about a mile to emerge in a different world! On your right low stone walls encircle the precincts of the former Abbey with the porter's lodge over the gate and on your left green lawns golden with daffodils in spring slope down the the river's edge. Beyond the walls there is a glimpse of the towers of Palace House, formerly the Abbey gatehouse, now the home of Lord Montagu whose ancestors bought the estate when the monasteries were dissolved in 1538.

Turn left to cross the mill dam.

2. Pass the former mill on the left and turn left beside the Montagu

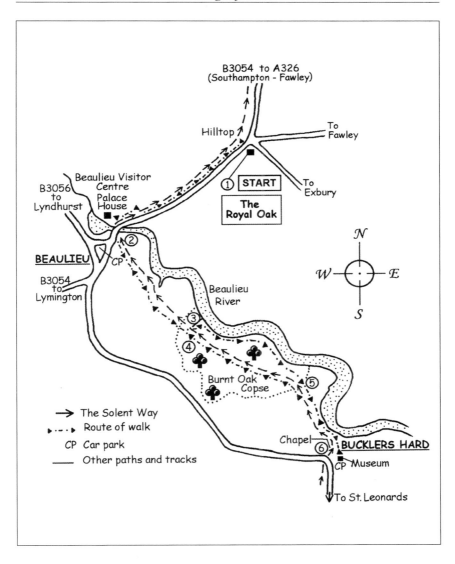

Arms. The track leads round the hotel which is on your right, through a gate and leads beside fields with the river a silver ribbon winding through woodlands in the distance. The track becomes a wide grassy path which slopes down to an inlet then rises to follow the edge of fields with a hedge on the left. Soon you will see Brickyard Cottage ahead and the former brickworks established in 1790 close to the river. Past the

43

cottage the path skirts another inlet, Baileys Hard. It was here that the first warship was built on the river, the *Salisbury* of 48 guns, by Richard Herring in 1696. During the last world war a wooden minesweeper was built here.

3. Just after a private gravel track joins on the left, the walk bears right. A few yards further on turn left for Bucklers Hard following the footpath sign. Now the Solent Way takes the straight track running through the woods ahead but an attractive path winds along the river bank which is the route of our walk. To find it, continue along the straight track for about 200 yards to cross a small stream.

4. Turn left towards the river over a wooden walkway and follow the path along the riverside in the footsteps of the monks and in later centuries those of the workers in the shipyards. Beyond the shoreline at low tide stretch banks of reed-fringed saltmarsh spiked with Townsend's grass, a form of cordgrass. Sea lavender turns the marsh purple in late summer. The path curves right as you leave Burnt Oak Copse to meet the gravel track on the right and the route of the Solent Way.

5. Continue in the direction of Bucklers Hard past the marina to a narrow road. Cross, and take the footpath a little to your left on the other side which leads you back to the river and Bucklers Hard village. Pass the remains of the old slipways. Turn right to walk up the street which runs between rows of cottages built of deep red handmade bricks set beyond wide expanses of grass. Trees for building our 'hearts of oak' were readily available in the Forest but at that time pine for decking had to be imported and stacked on the grass until needed.

Little seems to have changed in the village. Overlooking the water on your right is the Master Builder's house and if you look in the window of his study you will see the figure of the master builder himself, Henry Adams, discussing the plans of his latest warship with one of the Navy Board overseers. Further up the street is the tiny chapel dedicated to St Mary, formerly a school. Several of the cottages portray the lifestyle of 18th century villagers. A visit to the museum is a 'must'. It tells the whole story of Bucklers Hard with a reconstruction of the village inn complete with well-known figures of the time.

6. Retrace your steps to the entrance to Burnt Oak Copse (end of point 4) and either follow the riverside path or take the gravel woodland track.

The Beaulieu river at Bucklers Hard

You may like to explore Beaulieu village on your way back to Hilltop and the Royal Oak.

 SOLENT WAY: Bucklers Hard – Beaulieu – Hythe Pier (9 miles)

After the riverside walk the Solent Way crosses Beaulieu Heath to leave the New Forest. Although passing through an industrial area the route is surprisingly rural and there are splendid views of Southampton Water with its wealth of shipping.

Follow the return route of Walk 6 from the waterfront at Bucklers Hard, through Burnt Oak Copse, across the fields and through Beaulieu to Hilltop. Continue along the B3054 to meet the main road (A326) close to the roundabout at Dibden Purlieu. Before the roundabout, by the cattle grid, bear right (south-east) to follow the Forest edge with the A326 on the left for about 1½ miles to the next roundabout at Hardley. Just past the Hardley roundabout cross the A326 and keep straight on down the lane ahead past the Forest Home pub on your right. After about 100 yards go straight over the crossroads towards the Esso depot (Hythe Terminal). Continue for a few yards, then turn left along a footpath. The path doglegs right and left and becomes a country lane.

45

Feeding the ducks at Beaulieu

Pass a joining track on the left and when the main track curves right follow the lane leading straight ahead. Pass the Travellers' Rest pub and continue along the road – Hart Hill. Turn right at the next crossing track to the shore of Southampton Water.

The road bears left to follow the shoreline past extensive saltmarshes towards large grey sheds used for maintenance in the days of the flying boats. Keep straight on into Hythe and follow the signs to the ferry. This leaves from the end of the pier served by a narrow gauge railway. Now turn to Walk 7, page 51.

FACTFILE

Wilts and Dorset buses run to Beaulieu from Lymington and Hythe, stopping at Hilltop. Telephone: 01202 673555.

Beaulieu Visitor Centre (Abbey Ruins, Palace House, Motor Museum) is open every day, except Christmas Day, from 10 am to 5 pm or 7 pm depending on the season. Telephone: 01590 612345.

Bucklers Hard Maritime Museum. Open daily but times vary. Telephone for details: 01590 616203.

BY THE DARK WATER – A HIDDEN NEW FOREST VALLEY

(Solent Way: Hythe Pier – Southampton – Weston Point, Southampton Water)

The Bridge Tavern

Although the Solent Way runs through some beautiful areas of the New Forest these are mainly privately owned and the route is confined to rights-of-way. The route may alter in the future but in the meantime this walk, which is close to the Solent Way as it crosses Beaulieu Heath, will reveal a different New Forest where you can wander almost at will in a medieval landscape of heathland and commons, tree-shaded streams and ancient oak woods.

East of the Beaulieu river, another stream makes its way south to meet the Solent. This is the Dark Water, not as well known as the Beaulieu, but with a quiet charm all its own as it meanders down a thickly wooded valley. Overlooking the stream at Ipers Bridge you will find the ideal starting point for our walk, the Bridge Tavern. It is thought that this traditional Forest pub with its huge double brick fireplace and intriguing beamed doorways was originally several cottages possibly built around the early 1700s. Once you have visited this delightful friendly pub you will want to return.

It is important to arrive with a good appetite as the wide range of dishes on offer is really exceptional. Homemade steak and kidney pies and puddings are listed beside more exotic dishes such as stir-fried kangaroo with honey and ginger and breaded lobster tails. To follow, you might be tempted by a mouth-watering rum log with cream. Real ales are Wadworth 6X, Morland Old Speckled Hen and Ringwood Best Bitter. The house cider is Strongbow and there is a well-chosen selection of wines. In summer you can enjoy all these pleasures on the patio which overlooks the Dark Water valley.

Opening times in summer are from 11 am to 3 pm (Sunday 12 noon to 3 pm) and from 5.30 pm to 11 pm (Sunday 7 pm to 10.30 pm); in winter from 12 noon to 2.30 pm and from 6 pm to 11 pm (Sunday 7 pm to 10.30 pm). Meals are served from 12 noon to 2.30 pm (in winter to 2 pm) and from 6.30 pm to 9.30 pm (Sunday 7 pm to 9 pm). Telephone: 023 80892554.

- HOW TO GET THERE: The best approach is via the A326. Drive towards Fawley through Hardley and turn right, signed for Blackfield and Lepe. Continue to the traffic lights (just over ¼ mile) then turn right for Beaulieu. After just over a mile the road dips to cross the Dark Water at Ipers Bridge and the pub is on your left. Alternatively, take a bus from Hythe (see Factfile) and start the walk at point 4.
- PARKING: Patrons may leave cars in the Bridge Tavern car park but it is wise to have a word with the management first.
- LENGTH OF THE WALK: 4 miles. Map: OS Outdoor Leisure 22 New Forest (GR 424031).

THE WALK

1. Leave the front of the pub and turn right to cross Ipers Bridge and walk up the hill ahead. Look down over the meadows on the left and you will see they are ridged and embanked. In medieval times this was the site of Holbury Manor. 'Holbury' means a fortress in a hollow and there was a flourishing Roman settlement here.

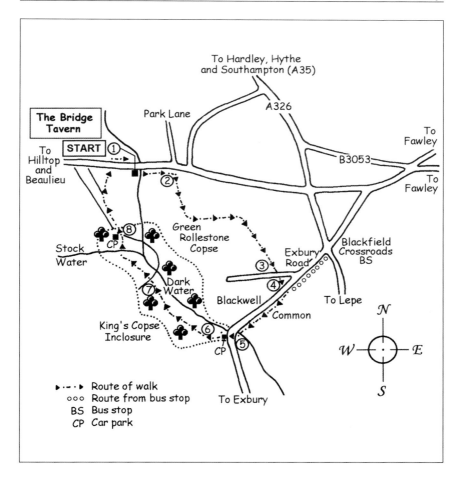

The Bridge Tavern

To Hardley, Hythe and Southampton (A35)

A326

Park Lane

To Hilltop and Beaulieu

START ①

To Fawley

B3053

To Fawley

②

Green Rollestone Copse

⑧

CP

Stock Water

Blackfield Crossroads BS

Exbury Road

③

④

To Lepe

Dark Water

⑦

Blackwell

King's Copse Inclosure

⑥

Common

CP ⑤

To Exbury

N

W ⊕ E

S

▶ ·· ▶ Route of walk
ooo Route from bus stop
BS Bus stop
CP Car park

2. At the top of the hill, opposite Park Lane, turn right following the bridleway sign. This leafy pathway, overlooking fields, running along the eastern boundary of the Forest, divides two contrasting worlds. Opposite the gates of Green Rollestone House the track turns left beside a wood on the right, thickly carpeted with bluebells in May. Go through a gate past a track on the right leading to a house and cross a lane. Keep ahead along a wide raised greenway firm underfoot and running in a determined fashion towards the old trading port near Lepe or Stone Point. I believe it is a continuation of the known ancient British track part of which can be seen in Fawley Inclosure. The greenway curves right and brings you after about ¾ mile to a lane.

The Dark Water in springtime

3. Cross the lane and keep straight on over the heath, Blackwell Common, to the Exbury road and turn right.

4. Follow the road towards the dark line of the woods of King's Copse Inclosure which clothe the Dark Water valley. Cross the bridge and climb the road ahead.

5. After about 50 yards turn right and cross the Dark Water car park. Take the woodland path ahead close to a fence on the embankment on your left. Go through a gate into King's Copse Inclosure.

6. Just beyond the gate the track divides. Take the right-hand path which traces the hillside with the Dark Water invisible as yet beneath a screen of willows and oaks. Keep to the main track ignoring all joining paths on the left.

7. When you come to a crosstrack – the track on the right leads down to a bridge over the stream – keep straight on along an attractive grassy path. Follow this as eventually it leads down to a bridge over Stock Water, a tiny stream flowing into the Dark Water. The fine naturalist and author W.H. Hudson arrived in England from Argentina in 1869 and rented Roydon Manor near Boldre. He spent much of his time in the Dark Water valley which he describes in his book *Hampshire Days*. In the sunlight, he notes, 'the water is the colour of old sherry from the red soil it flows over'.

Cross the bridge and climb the track ahead which bears left to a gate leading out of the Inclosure.

8. Keep straight on over King's Copse car park and follow the heathland path running at first to the right of the gravel track ahead. When this divides take the right-hand path to the road and turn right to return to the Bridge Tavern.

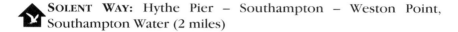

SOLENT WAY: Hythe Pier – Southampton – Weston Point, Southampton Water (2 miles)

From earliest times Southampton has been a port and centre of shipbuilding benefiting from a deep and easy approach, double high tides and convenient access to the Continent. This has left a rich legacy, some of which can be enjoyed on this short walk along the waterfront.

The Hythe ferry berths at the Town Quay. Walk past the complex of shops and restaurants and cross the main road to see part of Southampton's medieval walls adjoining the 15th century Watergate in Porter's Lane. Here merchants trading English wool for wines from the Mediterranean and spices and silks from the east paid their taxes. On the right the remains of a Norman merchant's house have been excavated. Turn right to cross the High Street and turn down Winkle Street. Walk under God's House Gate, built in the 13th century and named after a 12th century hospice for pilgrims. Adjoining is God's House Tower, built in the 15th century to protect the sluice gates which controlled the flow of water into the town moat. Now the buildings house a Museum of Archaeology with fascinating displays illustrating daily life in Southampton's three towns, Roman Clausentum, Saxon Hamwih and the medieval town.

Continue along Platform Road and Canute Road past South Western House. During Southampton's greatest days as the headquarters of the Royal Mail, Union Castle and Cunard steamship lines, this was the railway terminus hotel. Turn left into Royal Crescent, then right into Albert Road South. On your left stands Southampton's Hall of Aviation incorporating the R.J. Mitchell Museum which tells the story of Southampton as a centre for commercial aviation. Supermarine Aviation Works at Woolston built the Empire class flying boats, operated by Imperial Airways and BOAC. R.J. Mitchell, Supermarine's chief designer, worked on seaplanes to produce the Supermarine S6B which won the Schneider Trophy outright for Britain in 1931. Mitchell used the expertise he gained on seaplanes in his design for the Spitfire.

Climb the steps at the end of the road to cross the Itchen Bridge and descend the steps at the other side into Woolston. Bear right along Bridge Road, cross Portsmouth Road and continue down Victoria Road to Southampton Water at Weston Point. Now turn to Walk 8, page 57.

FACTFILE

This walk can be started from the Exbury road as it crosses Blackwell Common at point 4. Catch a Solent Blue line bus from Hythe for Lepe. Alight at the Blackfield crossroads and turn left along Exbury Road. Telephone: 023 80226235.

Museum of Archaeology. Open daily 10 am to 12 noon and 1 pm to 5 pm (Saturday to 4 pm); Sunday 2 pm to 5 pm. Telephone: 023 80224216/80632493.

Hall of Aviation. Open 10 am to 5 pm, Tuesday to Saturday. In the school holidays open additionally from 12 noon to 5 pm on Sunday and Monday. Telephone: 023 80635830.

WALK 8

ROYAL VICTORIA COUNTRY PARK, NETLEY ABBEY AND THE WESTWOOD

(Solent Way: Weston Point, Southampton Water – Royal
Victoria Country Park – Hamble Ferry)

The Prince Consort

This is an ideal family walk as there is something to please everyone. History comes alive in the romantic ruins of Netley Abbey and in the Royal Victoria Country Park, once the site of a great military hospital now a large landscaped area with a museum recreating life in Victorian times. The route follows the Solent Way as far as the pier where the wounded were ferried ashore then turns inland to explore Westwood Woodland Park. Here you step back in time 800 years and follow paths through pasture woodland little changed since it belonged to the monks of Netley Abbey.

Until the 19th century only the ruins of Netley Abbey overlooked the thickly wooded eastern shore of Southampton Water. But reaction to the horrors of the Crimean War led to the building of a great British Army hospital on the waterside. It was named after Queen Victoria who laid the foundation stone in 1856. She took a keen personal interest in the hospital and often visited the wards. A village grew up beside its gates and, of course, there had to be a convenient pub!

Our starting point is this splendidly Victorian inn, originally called 'The Army and Navy'. The name was changed to 'The Prince Consort' to honour the Queen's husband. Walk inside and enter Victorian England. Everything is in keeping with the time from the deep maroon drapes and carpeting to the elegant fireplace with its floral tiles. Apart from the spacious bar areas there is a large, beautifully appointed restaurant. Everyone receives a warm and friendly welcome and there is plenty of room for families. There are bar and snack menus which include tempting homemade soups, hot baguettes with a variety of interesting fillings – try the smoked salmon and cream cheese! – Cumberland sausage on garlic mash, and a range of 'specials'. Full meals available when we visited included the roast of the day, chicken breast stuffed with bacon and leeks and oven-cooked rainbow trout with citrus butter.

Real ales are Fuller's London Pride, Morland Old Speckled Hen and Gale's HSB. Cider is Strongbow and there is an extensive and popular wine list. The pub is open all week from 11 am to 11 pm; Sundays 12 noon to 10.30 pm. Food is available all day. The Prince Consort offers attractive accommodation in a separate cottage-style building. Telephone: 023 80452676.

- HOW TO GET THERE: To avoid driving through Southampton take the M27, leave at junction 8 and follow the signs for the Royal Victoria Country Park. Follow the sign close to Netley waterfront and turn left into Victoria Road. The pub is almost immediately on your left.
- PARKING: Clients are welcome to leave cars in the pub car park while they walk but have a word with the management first.
- LENGTH OF THE WALK: 4 miles. Map: OS Outdoor Leisure 22 New Forest (GR 456083).

THE WALK

1. Turn left from the front door of the Prince Consort and follow the road as it approaches Southampton Water on the right and the entrance to the Royal Victoria Country Park on the left. Just before the

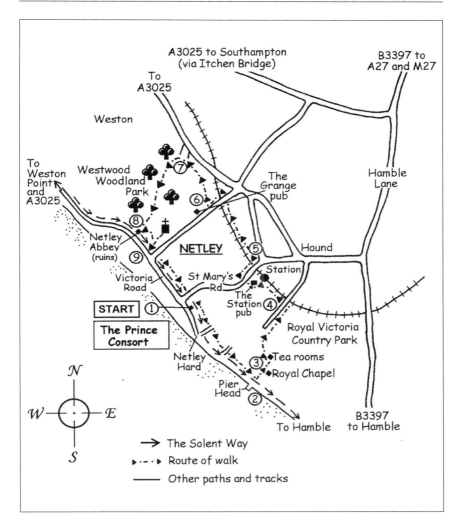

A3025 to Southampton
(via Itchen Bridge)

B3397 to
A27 and M27

To
A3025

Weston

To
Weston
Point
and
A3025

Westwood
Woodland
Park

⑦

⑥

⑧

The
Grange
pub

Hamble
Lane

Netley
Abbey
(ruins)

⑨

†

NETLEY

⑤

Hound

Victoria
Road

St Mary's
Rd

Station

The
Station
pub

④

START ①

**The Prince
Consort**

Netley
Hard

③

Tea rooms

Royal Chapel

Royal Victoria
Country Park

Pier
Head ②

N

W — ⊕ — *E*

S

B3397
to Hamble

To Hamble

→ The Solent Way

▶--·▶ Route of walk

—— Other paths and tracks

park entrance several streams have been channelled into a series of small lakes providing a haven for ducks and geese. Opposite is part of Netley Hard which dates from the 13th century. In the past it was the scene of great activity, including the famous Netley Regatta.

Follow the road into the park and keep straight ahead beneath the trees fringing the waterside for about ½ mile. The hospital was demolished in 1966 but the Royal Chapel with its conspicuous green dome has been preserved. And everywhere there are the beautiful trees and shrubs favoured by Victorian gardeners – Corsican, Scots and Monterey pines, holm oaks, cedars and viburnums.

2. When you come to the Pier Head leave the Solent Way and turn left to follow a gravel path to the chapel. From the platform in the dome you can enjoy a magnificent view of Southampton Water. Leave the chapel on your right and keep ahead to the narrow-gauge railway. Turn left and walk up to the park tea rooms, a large wooden building formerly the hospital YMCA.

3. With your back to the shore and the tea rooms on your right take the gravel footpath leading ahead between pine trees (with a car park at first close on your left) to a road. Bear right down the road to leave the park through Hound Gate. Note the gas lamp standard!

4. After about 100 yards turn left along a narrow footpath running along the top of a wooded valley then through a housing estate to Netley Station. Turn left, then bear right round the Station pub to St Mary's Road. Walk up to the railway bridge, cross, and take the footpath on the left.

5. Follow the path with the line on your left to Grange Road. Turn left to recross the line in the direction of the red-brick Grange pub.

6. Just before the pub turn right through the entrance to the Westwood Woodland Park. Follow the main track as it curves left over Grange Fields towards the woods. When you reach the trees and the track curves right, keep straight ahead along the narrow path into Bluebell Wood. You cross deep ditches, originally conduits dug by the monks to channel water to their fishponds, to a crossing path.

7. Turn left and follow this path, keeping straight ahead at all divisions through this lovely area known as 'Southampton's Secret Woodland'. Leave the park through an iron gate beside the entrance to Fountain Court.

8. Turn right and go through a gate on your left to stand high on an embankment and enjoy a spectacular view of the ruins of Netley Abbey set in a shallow valley shaded by huge oaks and beeches. Much of the graceful 13th century work remains, particularly the soaring arches and

The ruins of Netley Abbey

windows of the Abbey church. Bear left and walk down to explore the Abbey, then with the ruins on your right (an isolated building is on your left) cross the grass and go through a gate at the foot of a hill. Turn right then left up steps to a lane leading to Netley church on the left. Turn right to walk down to Victoria Road.

9. Bear left to walk through Netley, aptly described by Pevsner as a 'Victorian period piece', to return to the Prince Consort pub.

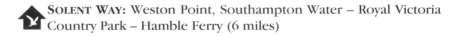

SOLENT WAY: Weston Point, Southampton Water – Royal Victoria Country Park – Hamble Ferry (6 miles)

The Way takes a closer look at the eastern shore of Southampton Water as it follows the waterside through the park then crosses part of Hamble Common, an area of unimproved grassland exceptionally rich in wildlife, to the ferry.

From Weston Point take the little path running beneath oak trees close to the shore and continue along the sea front and beach past Netley Castle, now vanished within a Victorian building. Bear left over the recreation ground to the road and pass the entrance to the ruins of

Netley Pond

Netley Abbey on your left. Follow the road and the signs for the Royal Victoria Country Park to the Prince Consort pub. Now follow the route of Walk 8 as far as the Pier Head (point 2). Keep straight on past the sailing club and dinghy park and follow the beach past the works of Aerostructures. During World War I Sir Edwin Alliott Verdon-Roe – the first Englishman to construct and fly his own aeroplane – established an aircraft factory here.

Approaching the BP terminal take the concrete pathway above the beach over an inlet and when the terminal fence turns left keep straight on along the edge of Hamble Common. Pass the first footpath sign on the left but turn left at the second post and follow a pleasant path through woodland to a lane. Keep ahead, then bearing a little right follow School Lane to the B3397 in Hamble village. Turn right and continue downhill to the quayside and the ferry. Now turn to Walk 9, page 64.

FACTFILE

Netley is served by First Southampton Buses, telephone: 023 80224854, and Solent Blue Line, telephone: 023 80618233. You could also start from Netley Station (point 4) which is on the main Southampton–Portsmouth line, telephone: 08457 484950.

Royal Victoria Country Park. Open all year, entry free. Chapel and tea rooms open from Easter to September. Telephone: 023 80455157.

Westwood Woodland Park. Open all year, entry free. For details of guided walks and special events ring the Park Office. Telephone: 023 80455157 ext.25.

WALK 9

HAMBLE AND BURSLEDON –
THE 'HOWARDS' WAY' WALK
(Solent Way: Hamble Ferry – Warsash Landing,
car park)

The Victory Inn

❧

The Solent Way glances only briefly at the Hamble river, as, hugging the coastline, it crosses over to Warsash and continues eastwards. But as you follow the route of this circular walk along the banks of this historic river, world famous as a yachting centre and still fringed with bird-haunted marshes and ancient oak woods, I am sure you will agree it richly deserves a closer look. Some of the scenery will be familiar if you were a fan of the TV series, 'Howard's Way'.

Hamble's fame as a yachting centre attracts many visitors but in spite of the crowds its narrow streets lined with 18th century houses have managed to retain their old world charm. And there could be no better haven for sailors – or walkers – as beside the High Street and the picturesque alley leading down to the quay you will find no fewer than five pubs! One of the oldest, the starting point of this walk, is named after Nelson's famous flagship HMS *Victory*. The Victory Inn was already over 100 years old when Nelson led his twenty-two ships of the line against the combined French and Spanish fleet at Trafalgar. As you sit in the oak-beamed bar you feel you could well be on board a man o'war. Reminders of naval battles surround you and there is a magnificent mural depicting the battle of Trafalgar. More recent times are recalled by a table top on which commandos about to embark for France on D-Day have carved their names.

Apart from a warm welcome and comfortable surroundings you will find an excellent choice of dishes on the menu. Among the snacks are 'Ploughman's Platters', filled jacket potatoes and freshly baked baguettes. More substantial meals when we were there included tasty homemade pies and Fajitas – strips of chicken breast or fillet beef coated with the pub's secret Fajita spices. Fresh fish is a speciality of the house. Real ales are Brakspear, Flowers, Fuller's and Wadworth 6X and there is an excellent wine list.

The pub is open throughout the week from 11 am to 11 pm (Sundays 12 noon to 10.30 pm). Food is served on Monday to Saturday from 12 noon to 2.30 pm and 7 pm to 9 pm and on Sunday from 12 noon to 8 pm. Telephone: 023 80453105.

> • HOW TO GET THERE: Approach via the M27 and exit at junction 8. Follow the signs for Hamble and drive into the village where you will find a car park in The Square on your left.
> • PARKING: In the large public car park off Hamble High Street.
> • LENGTH OF THE WALK: 6½ miles. Map: OS Outdoor Leisure 22 New Forest. (GR 483068).

THE WALK

1. Turn left from the car park and walk towards the top of the narrow street running steeply downhill to the waterfront. Overhanging the roadside on your right you pass the 17th century Old House, half-timbered and infilled with herringbone brickwork. Walk down the street to the quay, passing the Victory on your left. From seats on the quayside there is a splendid view of the river. Yachts built to the very latest design, ocean racers, old-timers and fishing boats are mirrored together in the still water against a background of woods and marshes.

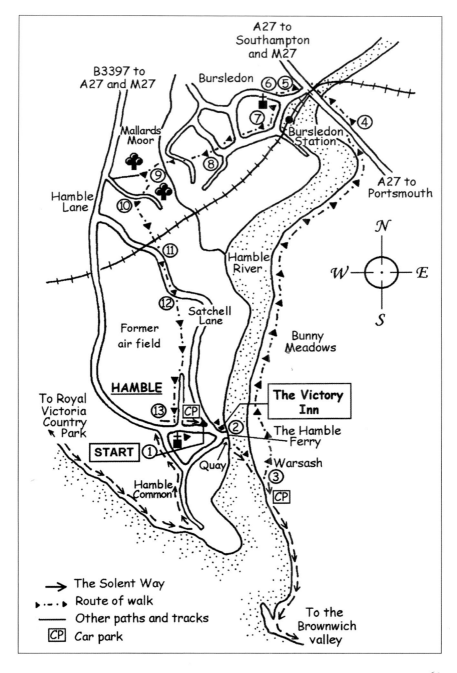

The ferry over the Hamble river

2. Take the ferry across the river to the Warsash ferry landing and walk up to the raised footpath. Here we leave the Solent Way.

3. Turn left to follow the east bank of the river upstream. The path crosses saltmarshes and mudflats interlaced with creeks, happy hunting grounds for waders, especially redshanks, dunlins and curlews. Rock pipits hop along the shoreline. The brackish lagoons inland – known as Bunny Meadows – are specially rich in wildlife. Look for a watchful heron or perhaps the iridescent blue flash of a kingfisher. Keep to the riverside path for over 2 miles past all paths on the right. Walk through Universal Shipyards and join the footpath again just past the wooden office buildings. As you approach Swanwick you meet a lane. Keep straight on to the main road, the A27.

4. Bear left to cross the bridge, go under the railway bridge and turn almost immediately left along the road signed for Bursledon Station.

5. When the road divides bear right up Church Lane to the little church of St Leonard on the left. This attractive church with its small half-timbered tower and long wooden porchway was built by monks from Hamble Priory in the early 13th century. It is known as the shipbuilders' church and inside is a memorial to George Parsons who built HMS *Elephant*, Nelson's flagship.

6. Take the narrow footpath running downhill past steps on the right leading up to the churchyard. When the path divides take the right-hand path through a gate to a lane in Old Bursledon. Continue uphill and at the fork bear right to pass Greywell, the first of many elegant 18th century houses built of grey and red bricks from the local works. (The works have been restored and are signed off the A27.) At the next junction we turn right but you might like to make a short detour left to the railway bridge where you can look down on the Elephant boatyard where the famous man o' war was built along with many others throughout the 14th, 15th and 16th centuries.

7. Turn right as directed above and follow the High Street. On the right there are glimpses of the lower reaches of the river winding to the sea and the hills of the Isle of Wight. Keep straight on at the next junction past the Vine pub, cross the top of Salterns Lane and follow Kew Lane for a few yards until it begins to curve right.

8. Take the narrow footpath on the left running close to the wall of a house and follow it downhill to a lane. Keep ahead along the lane until it curves right. Now keep straight on along the footpath ahead, cross a track and continue ahead to cross a wooden footbridge and enter the oak and beech woods of Mallards Moor.

9. Climb up through the trees and at the division bear left along the main track which traces the top of a wooded hillside to meet a lane. Bear right along the lane for only a few yards and just before the lane begins to curve right look carefully for a footpath on the left (no sign) which runs to the right of a high wire fence.

10. Turn left along this path with the green tower of the chapel of the Royal Victoria Park directly ahead. The path leads you over a railway bridge to meet Satchell Lane.

11. Bear left along the lane for a little over ¼ mile. The land on the right was once part of the airfield of the College of Air Training established in 1960. The lane bends left and after about 30 yards look carefully for a footpath sign on the right.

12. Turn right and follow the path which eventually runs through housing estates and brings you to the road opposite Hamble's 12th

Hamble Quay

century priory church built by Benedictine monks from the Abbey of Tiron in France who were granted land here by the Bishop of Winchester. The Hamble river was famous for its oysters and the Prior would send each year in Lent 20,000 of these delectable shellfish to the monks of St Swithins in Winchester. In return the six monks in Hamble received 21 loaves and 42 flagons of ale each week.

13. Turn left along the road to return to your car and the Victory Inn.

 Solent Way: Hamble Ferry – Warsash landing, car park (½ mile)

A chance to take things easy and enjoy one of the south's most attractive rivers!

Take the ferry ride over the Hamble river and walk up to the raised footpath on the Warsash shore. Turn right to walk the few yards to a car park. Now turn to Walk 10, page 70.

FACTFILE

Hamble is served by Solent Blue Line buses, telephone: 023 80618233 and First Southampton Buses, telephone: 023 80224854. The walk can also be started from Bursledon Station (join at point 7) on the main Southampton–Portsmouth line, telephone: 08457 484950.

The Hamble–Warsash ferry runs on demand on Monday to Friday from 7 am to 5 pm and on Saturday and Sunday from 9 am to 4 pm.

HOOK-WITH-WARSASH NATURE RESERVE

(Solent Way: Warsash Landing, car park –
Brownwich valley)

The Rising Sun

❦

Most of this walk explores the richly contrasting scenery of the Hook-with-Warsash Nature Reserve. From the shingle banks beside Southampton Water paths lead over reclaimed pasture, by lagoons and freshwater lakes and through beautiful oak and beech woods, home for badgers and deer. A wealth of birdlife includes seabirds along the shore, kingfishers and warblers around the lakes and woodpeckers and nuthatches in the woods.

Today, yachting is important at Warsash but the quay presents a less crowded scene than Hamble. The row of sturdy knapped flint cottages leading down to the waterfront still conveys the atmosphere of the days when the village was a small fishing community. It was noted for its crabs and lobsters, brought in specially constructed 'crabbers' from Brittany, Ireland and the West Country. The seafood was stored in tanks the remains of which you can still see at low tide. But if you enjoy fish straight from the boats there is no need to despair! Just drop in to the Rising Sun pub close to the start of our walk. The origins of this large popular pub can be traced back to 1784 when 'a messuage and malthouse' were rented to a Mr George Parsons for 3d per year. The wooden or quarry tiled floors and wood panelled walls are part of the old structure.

High quality seafood is a speciality and includes wild salmon from the seas around Alaska and moules marinière. Among other dishes on the menu when we were there was 'Drunken Duck' (he is partial to Grand Marnier) and Scottish Aberdeen Angus beef. The Rising Sun also specialises in Mediterranean cuisine. A wide range of 'Lite Bites' is on offer too. Real ales are 6X, Pedigree, Flowers and Ringwood. The pub is close to the waterside and there are splendid river views particularly from the upstairs non-smoking restaurant.

Opening times are from 11 am to 11 pm every day except Sunday when the hours are from 12 noon to 10.30 pm. Meals are served from 12 noon to 2.15 pm and from 7 pm to 9.15 pm. Telephone: 01489 576898.

• HOW TO GET THERE: Exit the M27 at junction 8. At the roundabout take the A27 south-east, signed for Fareham. Continue to Sarisbury and turn right down Barnes Lane following the sign for Warsash. At the junction bear right down Brook Lane to the next roundabout where you turn right again along Shore Road following the sign for the D-Day memorial to the waterfront. The road curves right past the Rising Sun. Ignore the car park opposite (4 hours limit) and continue round the corner to the large car park immediately on your left.

• PARKING: The free car park on the corner of Shore Road.

• LENGTH OF THE WALK: 4½ miles. Map: OS Explorer 119 Meon Valley (GR 489062).

THE WALK

1. Turn right from the car park entrance and follow Shore Road as it curves left along the waterfront. In the car park opposite the Rising Sun is a D-Day memorial commemorating the departure of British and Allied naval commando units from the Hamble river for the

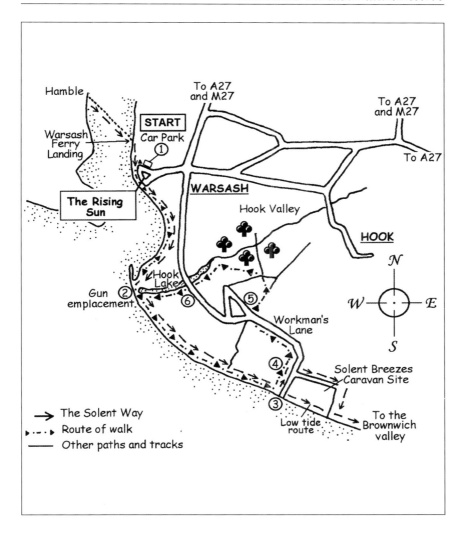

Normandy beaches on the night of 5th June 1944. Three thousand commandos embarked on 36 landing craft of HMS *Tormentor* based nearby. A plaque on the wall of the Rising Sun also records the occasion.

Pass the pub on your left and continue along the shore path which rises to trace the top of a grassy embankment then runs down to follow the shore once more, passing Warsash College of Maritime Studies. At the end of the college's jetty lifeboats are poised ready for the cadets to practise lowering and boarding.

The path bears right to cross the sluice gates and dam over the Hook channel. Before the construction of the dam at the end of the 18th century the river was the harbour for Newtown, then a larger port than Hamble, with shipbuilding and repairing yards. The village was destroyed by William Hornby, a retired Governor of Bombay, who built a replica of Government House at Hook and decided to dam the river to make an ornamental lake. The house was burnt down but the grounds remain forming the wilderness of lagoons and reed beds now part of the Nature Reserve.

Ahead a shingle spit curls round the coast to form a hook – hence the name. It supports many interesting plants including sea rocket with its clusters of tiny lilac-coloured flowers, yellow horned poppy and the striped pink and white bells of sea bindweed.

2. The shore path curves left past a former gun emplacement and a footpath on the left which is our return route. Continue past Hook Links on the left, rough grassland once the site of a Roman saltworks. Continue along the beach to Solent Breezes Caravan Park.

3. Turn left along Workman's Lane to pass the caravan site on your right. The name of the lane recalls the fact that a hundred years ago a factory stood here which manufactured alkali by distilling wood ash.

Sluice gates and dam over Hook channel

The D-Day Memorial on Warsash Quay

4. When the track bends right we leave the Solent Way, which turns right. For the circular walk, keep straight ahead over a stile following Workman's Lane as it curves left to a T-junction.

5. Turn right and continue for about ¼ mile. Now look carefully for a grassy path on your left (no sign) leading down to an entrance into woods by a green notice board. Turn left to follow this to the woods and bear left through a small wooden gate in front of the notice board for Hook Valley. Take the right-hand of the two paths immediately after the gate. This becomes a beautiful terraced way along the top of a steep valley. Deep in the valley is a dense jungle of alder and willow rising to slopes covered with birch, ash, elm, maple and holly. Old oaks and beeches overhang the path.

Bear right past a footpath on the left to leave the woods and walk down a lane to a road.

6. Cross the road and go through a gate to follow a hedged footpath beside a reed-filled lagoon to join our outbound route to the left of the gun emplacement. Turn right to retrace your steps to the pub and your car.

Our path through Hook Woods

SOLENT WAY: Warsash Landing, car park – Brownwich valley (4 miles)

A beautiful stretch of the Way beside the Hamble estuary leading to the Brownwich valley, close to the Meon shore.

From the car park follow the route of Walk 10 as far as Solent Breezes Caravan Park (point 2). At low tide you can continue past the park on your left along the beach. Otherwise follow the route of Walk 10 and turn left up Workman's Lane to point 4. Leave the pub walk route here and turn right. Follow the track to a sign on your right indicating a path which eventually leads you back to the clifftop east of the caravan park. Continue along the clifftop path for about a mile enjoying wonderful views over the Solent to the Isle of Wight hills. The Way descends into the shallow valley of the Brownwich stream. Now turn to Walk 11, page 75.

FACTFILE
Warsash is served by First Provincial buses. Telephone: 01329 232208 and 023 92862412.

THE MEON SHORE – HILL HEAD HARBOUR AND TITCHFIELD HAVEN

(Solent Way: Brownwich valley – Hill Head –
Gosport Ferry) PO 14 3JR

The Osborne View

01329 664623   Food 12-930

*After the construction of a sea wall and one-way tidal flaps across
the estuary of the Meon river in 1611 by the third Earl of Southampton,
the area developed into a freshwater marsh including wet meadows,
dense reed beds, lagoons and a canal. Now the Titchfield Haven Nature
Reserve, it is exceptionally rich in wildlife. We start close to the dam at
Hill Head and follow the canal through the reserve to Titchfield village.
The return route follows the Brownwich valley to the sea and finishes,
with a superb clifftop ramble.*

Tiny Hill Head Harbour is one of the most attractive places on the coast. It is a world of small boats. A few yachts bob at moorings and the rest form a colourful jumble on the beach. From the sandstone cliffs framing the harbour there are wonderful views to the Isle of Wight, left to the open water of Spithead and right over the Solent to the entrance to Southampton Water. So there could be no better start for this pub walk than the Osborne View. It is built on the clifftop with bars and restaurants at several levels all offering splendid sea views. Here, in warm and comfortable surroundings, you will enjoy excellent food and drink. It comes as no surprise to discover that during World War I the pub became the favourite rendezvous of members of the Special Boat Squadron billeted in the village. They were looked after by the landlady, a motherly figure whom they affectionately termed 'Aunt Em'. A notice board gives details of some of their less respectable activities!

Real ales are Badger Best, Tanglefoot and IPA and a selection with splendid names from a local brewery at the Gribble Inn – Plucking Pheasant, Pig's Ear and Fursty Ferret. Gale's country wines are on offer and the cider is Blackthorn. Fish specials on the extensive menu when we were there included fillet of bream and salmon and among the meat dishes was a delicious turkey, ham and mushroom pie.

Opening hours on Monday to Saturday are 11 am to 11.30 pm. Food is served from 12 noon to 2.30 pm and 6 pm to 9.30 pm. Sunday hours are 12 noon to 11 pm and food is served all day. Telephone: 01329 664623.

• **HOW TO GET THERE:** Exit the M27 at junction 9 (Fareham West) and follow the A27 towards Titchfield. At the second roundabout take the third exit, St Margaret's Lane, for about ½ mile to a T-junction. Turn left for a few yards then turn right down Posbrook Lane, signed 'Meon', to head south. The lane turns sharp left over the canal. Continue past Hill Head Harbour for about ¼ mile to the Osborne View on your right and the car park on your left.

• **PARKING:** Patrons may leave their cars in the Osborne View car park at Hill Head but it is wise to have a word with the management first.

• **LENGTH OF THE WALK:** 8½ miles (easy walking). Map: OS Explorer 119 Meon Valley (GR 540022).

THE WALK

1. Turn left from the front door of the pub and after a few yards turn left again down a slip road to a path beside the beach. Bear right past beach huts and bear left round Hillhead Sailing Club. A roadside path leads over the dam across the harbour to a parking area. Bear left to a path on the seaward side of the low sea wall and continue with the parking area on your right and railings on your left. When the railings cease cross the road and go through the left-hand of two small wooden gates leading into the Titchfield Haven Nature Reserve.

2. Bear left along the footpath with the road on your left. Shortly, the path curves right. Continue for about 300 yards to a narrow path on the left.

3. Turn left to the canal bank. At this point the road ahead turns left over the original sea lock completed in 1611 as part of the Earl's plan to divert water from the Meon and drain the estuary. As a navigable channel the canal was a failure but today the towpath provides a splendid walk. Turn right to follow the towpath with the canal always on your left for over 2 miles to Titchfield. On your right you have a good view over the nature reserve. Cross a road and continue to a small bridge on your left leading to St Peter's church. In the days before the dam, when Titchfield was a flourishing port on a wide estuary, barges tied up at wharves close by.

4. Cross the bridge and find time if you can to visit the superb church famous for its early Anglo-Saxon porch and magnificent 16th century monument to the second Earl of Southampton and his parents. From the porch walk straight ahead up Church Street, cross Titchfield High Street and walk up West Street to meet St Margaret's Lane opposite West Hill Park School. Turn left to the road junction at Coach Hill.

5. Turn right to follow Common Lane to a T-junction. (Ignore the footpath on the left.)

6. Bear left (cut the corner along the pavement on the right of the road) and after about 300 yards turn left along Hook Lane to the car park at the entrance to Chilling Coastal area. This 1,000 acres of farmland is carefully managed to encourage wildlife.

7. Turn left beside the car park and follow the path which crosses farmland at first then traces the edge of the woods sloping down to the Brownwich Stream on your left and runs beside the western side of Brownwich Pond.

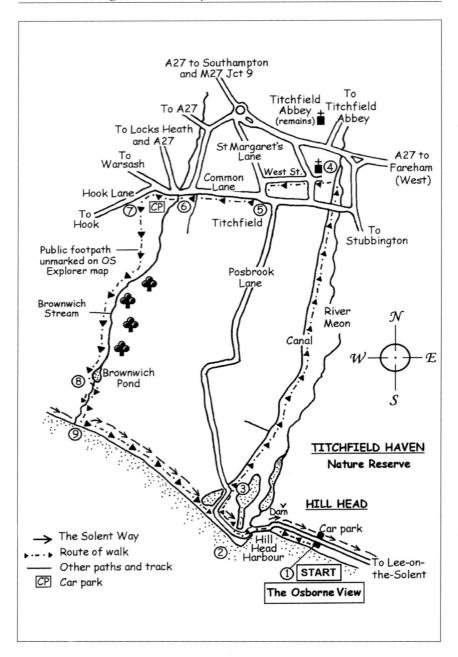

Titchfield

8. Just past the pond bear left following the main track towards a gate. Beside the gate turn right down some steps along a narrow path. At a crosspath bear right to cross the Brownwich Stream. Shortly, recross the stream and continue with the stream on your right to emerge on the beach. Turn left over the bridges.

9. Walk along the beach passing a footpath on your left. After about 50 yards bear left up the cliff and follow the path east along the clifftop. The path descends and runs behind beach huts to the road. Cross over, and bear right along the footpath to leave the reserve through the next gate. Retracing the pub walk route, cross the road and follow the path to the right of the low sea wall round Hill Head, past the beach huts. Turn left up the slip road to return to your car.

SOLENT WAY: Brownwich valley – Hill Head – Gosport Ferry (11 miles).

This is a busy but interesting section of the Way with fine views all along the coast, especially from the high earth embankments surrounding Fort Gilkicker, one of the ring of forts strengthened by Palmerston in the mid 19th century to protect Portsmouth Harbour.

Follow the route of Walk 11 from point 9 but do not turn left up the slip road. Keep straight ahead to follow the sea wall and beach. Approaching Lee-on-the-Solent make a slight deviation left then right to pass the naval hovercraft slipway serving HMS *Daedalus*, the Fleet Air Arm's Training establishment. Continue along Lee-on-the-Solent sea front as far as the dinghy park. Turn left, then right to the corner of Portsmouth Road then bear right to return to the shore. Turn left to follow the beach round Browndown Ranges and continue to Fort Gilkicker. Walk round the seaward side of the fort, then turn left to follow a path over the golf course with a lake on your right to a T-junction. Bear right along Fort Road which curves left to meet Haslar Road. Turn right and follow Haslar Road past the entrance to the Royal Navy Submarine Museum. Cross Haslar Bridge, then bear a little right along a very pleasant footpath along the Gosport Lines, ramparts designed by Sir Bernard de Gomme in 1660, to the ferry terminal. Now turn to Walk 12, page 81.

FACTFILE

Hill Head is served by First Provincial buses. Telephone: 01329 232208 and 023 92862412.

Titchfield Abbey was remodelled as a stately home after the Dissolution by Thomas Wriothesley, later the first Earl of Southampton. The third Earl was Shakespeare's patron and it is possible the first performance of *Romeo and Juliet* took place in the Tithe Barn. The imposing gatehouse remains, now owned by English Heritage. Open Good Friday to 30th September 10 am to 1 pm and 2 pm to 6 pm.

Royal Navy Submarine Museum. Offers a unique opportunity to be guided by submariners around the submarine HMS *Alliance*. Open every day from 10 am to 4.30 pm. Telephone: 023 92529217.

Titchfleld Haven Nature Reserve. The Information Centre is at Hill Head Harbour. For permits to join a guided tour write to: The Naturalist Warden, Haven Cottage, Cliff Road, Hill Head, Fareham, Hants or telephone: 01329 662145.

SPICE ISLAND AND SOUTHSEA COMMON

(Solent Way: Gosport Ferry – Historic Ships –
Old Portsmouth – Southsea Castle)

The Wellington

*T*he Point is a small peninsula between a natural inlet, the Camber, and the entrance to Portsmouth Harbour. It is also called by a much more evocative name – Spice Island. From the Grand Parade at the foot of Old Portsmouth High Street we explore this historic close-packed area. In the past it was outside the city limits and became a favourite place for sailors to row ashore and relax with a choice of 40 alehouses and inns! The route joins the Solent Way to follow the coast to Southsea Castle then turns inland to return past some of Southsea's elegant Regency-style terraces.

Portsmouth's long history as a naval base dates from the 15th century when Henry VII established the earliest known dry dock close to the present site of HMS *Victory*. Many famous sailors have trod its streets. But the Grand Parade, where we start this walk, was the heart of Fortress Portsmouth, the military town, fortified by Edward III during the Hundred Years' War. It was the scene of all ceremonial occasions and the centre of all the town's social activities. So perhaps I may be forgiven for choosing a pub that commemorates a great soldier, the Duke of Wellington.

The Wellington is a friendly, family run hostelry, popular with locals and visitors alike. Its Georgian-style windows overlook the entrance to Spice Island. A welcoming bar area leads into an attractive restaurant. Comfortable wooden seating and subdued lighting contribute to the pleasantly relaxed atmosphere. A highly professional chef produces excellent home-cooked meals including fish straight from the boats. If fish is your passion, try their whole grilled lemon sole! Other dishes might include chicken in tarragon sauce, King prawns in filo pastry and steak, ale and mushroom pudding. A wide range of bar snacks is also available. Real ales are 6X, Young's Special and a guest ale. In fine weather you can enjoy your meal or drink in the charming patio garden.

Opening times are from 11 am to 11 pm every day and food is served between 12 noon and 2 pm. On Wednesday, Thursday, Friday and Saturday evenings food is also served between 6.30 pm and 9.30 pm. It is wise to book your table beforehand, particularly at weekends. Telephone: 023 92818965.

> • HOW TO GET THERE: From the M27 take the M275 and follow the signs for Old Portsmouth and the Historic Ships. At the dockyard entrance turn left along The Hard. The road bears left to follow St George's Road to a roundabout. Take the third exit down Old Portsmouth High Street past the cathedral on your right. Just before the road turns right in front of the ramparts turn left to the parking area in Grand Parade.
> • PARKING: In the Grand Parade, Old Portsmouth.
> • LENGTH OF THE WALK: 4 miles. Map: OS Explorer 119 Meon Valley (GR 631993).

THE WALK

1. With houses on your left and the ramparts on your right walk past the open area on your right where the military garrison's guard house once stood. Just past this area, turn right to walk up onto the ramparts,

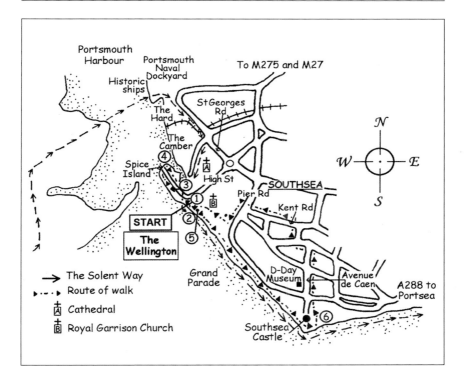

a sequence of gun batteries and towers which formed Old Portsmouth's harbour defences. You are standing on the Saluting Platform, a splendid viewpoint. Ahead, across the Solent, Bembridge and Ryde are sheltered by the Isle of Wight hills. Looking west a line of ramparts leads to the Round Tower, built by order of Henry V. Eastwards, protecting Spithead, are Lord Palmerston's four sea forts, Spitbank, Horse Sand, No Man's Land and St Helen's.

2. Turn right and follow the ramparts leaving the 15th century Square Tower on your right and follow the gun battery platform towards the Round Tower. On your left waves break on the narrow shingle beach where once sailors would draw up their boats and armies embark. Continue into the Round Tower through the arches and descend a flight of steps on your right to street level. Turn right to Broad Street to enter Spice Island.

3. Turn left for just a few yards, then turn left again down a narrow

79

The Point or 'Spice Island'

entry passing Capstan House on your right. Bear right along narrow
cobbled Tower Street between 17th century cottages and Captain's
House where William Wylie painted the *Battle of Trafalgar*.

Follow the next street, bearing a little left to Bath Square and passing
the original bath house, Quebec House, to the public hard on the tip of
Spice Island. All kinds of ships pass close by from modern warships in
their uniform grey and cross-channel ferries, to the colourful little
fishing boats chugging in and out of the Camber.

4. Turn right along Broad Street past the Spice Island pub on your
right and continue to Seager's Court on your left. Turn left to make
a short detour to enjoy a view of the Camber, then follow Broad Street
to the Square Tower at the foot of Old Portsmouth High Street, passing
the Sally Port, an opening in the defences through which as the plaque
states 'naval heroes innumerable have embarked to fight their country's
battles'. Climb the steps to the left of the Square Tower to join the Solent
Way and bear left.

5. Continue along the outer wall with the moat and Long Curtain on
your left. The walk continues past Southsea Common. Leave the Sea

Life Centre on your left and follow the sea front to Southsea Castle. Here the circular walk leaves the Solent Way.

6. With the castle on your left continue a few yards further then bear left up steps. Bear left again to walk down to the road leading to the castle entrance. Bear right away from the castle along Avenue de Caen past the D-Day Museum. Cross the road and continue along Palmerston Road. In front of the pedestrian precinct bear left for a few yards then turn right into Portland Road. Shortly you will pass Portand Terrace, a beautiful crescent reminiscent of Bath, designed by Thomas Ellis Owen.

7. Turn left to follow Kent Road to its junction with Pier Road. Bear left along Pier Road to a footpath on the right. Turn right to follow this footpath past Lord Nelson's statue and over Governor's Green. Do visit the Royal Garrison church on your right. It was once part of the Domus Dei, a shelter for travellers and pilgrims. Bombed in the last war, the 13th century chancel remains a consecrated church. The Grand Parade and your car are directly ahead. To visit the pub cross the Grand Parade to Old Portsmouth High Street and turn left. The pub is on the corner.

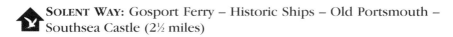 **SOLENT WAY:** Gosport Ferry – Historic Ships – Old Portsmouth – Southsea Castle (2½ miles)

This section of the Way presents a splendid opportunity to visit the Naval Dockyard museum and the Historic Ships – HMS Victory, HMS Warrior and the hull of Henry VIII's favourite warship the Mary Rose. From the Square Tower the route follows Walk 12 along Old Portsmouth ramparts to Southsea Castle.

Cross by ferry to Portsmouth Hard. Turn left to the entrance to the Naval Dockyard if you wish to visit the Museum and Historic Ships, then retrace your steps and walk up the road from the ferry landing. Bear slightly right to continue to the left of the railway to Ordnance Road. Turn right, then right again under the bridge. Bear right once more beside the wall of HMS *Vernon* and follow the wall as it leads right past the gates of HMS *Nelson*. Cross the approach to the Isle of Wight ferry and keep straight on down White Hart Road. Cross the road at the end and climb the ramparts ahead. Turn left to walk past the Square Tower and follow the route of Walk 12 from point 5 to Southsea Castle. Now turn to Walk 13, page 87.

FACTFILE

Portsmouth is well served by buses; for Stagecoach Coastline telephone: 01903 237661, for First Provincial telephone: 023 92862412. Rail enquiries: 08457 484950.

For Gosport Ferry times telephone: 023 92524551.

Portsmouth Naval Dockyard, including the Historic Ships and Royal Naval Museum, is open from November to February 10.30 am to 5.30 pm and from March to October 10 am to 6 pm. Telephone: 023 92433050.

Southsea Castle, built by Henry VIII in 1544, has been a military fortress for over 400 years but has never fired a shot in anger. Open daily from March to October 10 am to 5.30 pm, and from November to February 10 am to 4.30 pm. Telephone: 023 92827261.

D-Day Museum houses the remarkable Overlord Embroidery. For opening times and information telephone: 023 92827261.

While in Portsmouth take the opportunity to visit the Spinnaker Tower which soars 170 metres above Gunwharf Quays. The views over the harbour are magnificent. On a clear day it is possible to see over 23 miles. Opening times are Sunday to Friday 10 am to 5 pm; Saturday 10 am to 10 pm. These times can vary so for up-to-date information and admission prices telephone: 023 92857520.

The statue of Nelson, Portsmouth

WALK 13

WORLD OF THE WILD GEESE – FARLINGTON MARSHES

(Solent Way: Southsea Castle – Portsea Island –
Farlington Marshes, north-east)

The Compass Rose

The lonely expanse of Farlington Marshes, stretching into the northern waters of Langstone Harbour, is one of the finest nature reserves on the south coast. It is especially magical during the winter months when flocks of Brent geese arrive from the Arctic to feed on the saltings and rough pastures. Apart from the wealth of birdlife attracted by the tidal harbour, a wide variety of other habitats include a lagoon, freshwater streams and extensive reed beds. The Solent Way takes a harbourside footpath along the shore of Portsea Island before joining the route of the walk.

Langstone Harbour was once a coastal plain. It was flooded by rising sea levels as the ice melted over 12,000 years ago. The shallow waters almost dry out at low tide and in the past the harbour's few narrow creeks were the haunt of smugglers and pirates. Today they provide pleasant anchorages for small boats. So what better name could we have for the pub at the start of this walk than the Compass Rose? It would be easy to miss this friendly pub tucked away in Anchorage Park, a large estate built on the site of Portsmouth's former airport in the north-east corner of Portsea Island. Bright, spacious and airy the Compass Rose is a real 'community' pub with plenty of room for everyone and a warm welcome for families. Although the building is modern, the pub has a relaxed, traditional atmosphere with comfortable wooden furnishings and reminders of ships and the sea decorating the walls. There is a large bar area and a separate non-smoking restaurant.

Real ales are HSB, Ringwood, Bass and Courage and there is a good selection of wines. Home-cooking is strongly featured on the menu which includes excellent meat pies made in the old-fashioned way with shortcrust pastry. Game dishes such as wild boar, venison and ostrich are popular. Among fish options when we called were spicy swordfish and crispy fried scampi. The bar menu offers a wide range of snacks and lighter meals. A help-yourself buffet is served on Thursday evenings. You can choose from Indian, Chinese or Mexican dishes and eat as much as you like. Perfect for hungry walkers!

Outside there is a secluded beer garden and a walled play area for children. Opening times are from 11 am to 11 pm during the week and from 12 noon to 8.30 pm on Sundays. Meals are served on weekdays from 12 noon to 2.30 pm and 6 pm to 9.30 pm and all day on Sundays from 12 noon to 8.30 pm. Telephone: 023 92673037.

• HOW TO GET THERE: Leave the A27 southwards along the A2030, signed 'Southsea', to cross the bridge over Ports Creek. After about ½ mile take the first road on the right, Anchorage Road, just past Safeway. Drive round the roundabout and turn left into the car park. The Compass Rose is to the left of the store.

• PARKING: In the large car park opposite the pub, shared with Safeway.

• LENGTH OF THE WALK: 4½ miles. Map: OS Explorer 119 Meon Valley (GR 672035).

THE WALK

1. Turn left from the entrance to the car park to return to the A2030.

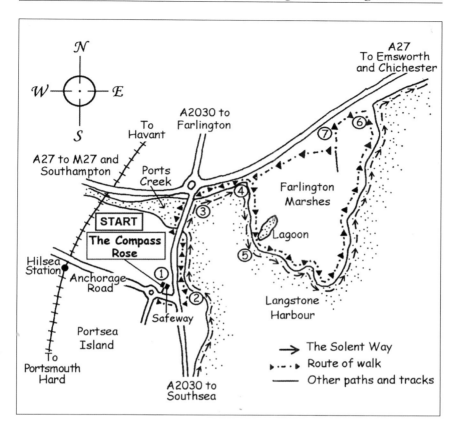

Cross the road and follow the lane ahead for just a few yards. Then bear left over the grass to join the route of the Solent Way as it runs beside the western shore of Langstone Harbour and turn left.

2. Follow the path to the bridge over Ports Creek. Cross the bridge, turn right, then almost immediately right again following the sign for Farlington Marshes.

3. Walk over the grass from the parking area to the sea wall and turn left along the wall with the wide expanse of Langstone Harbour on your right. At high tide the water laps the wall and fronds of eel grass – zostera – wave beneath it. As the water recedes it leaves behind a green algae. Both are favourite foods of Brent geese, recognisable by their black heads and necks and small white nick behind each cheek.

At the end of the parking area bear left for a few yards before turning right past the reserve entrance to rejoin the sea wall.

4. The low-lying pastures on your left are the oldest part of the reserve, probably enclosed 2,000 years ago. Continue across the line of the Old Bank, the ancient sea wall, to follow the path along the present wall built to enclose the marshes for rough grazing in the 18th century.

The path leads by a small lagoon. The salty areas sloping down to the lagoon are covered in mats of glasswort, vivid red in winter, sea asters, mud rushes and saltmarsh grass. Higher slopes have dense thickets of sedges, home for reed-warblers and reed-buntings and in autumn and early winter you may see bearded tits, lovely little birds with tawny orange bodies and long tails flying over the reeds on rapidly whirring wings. In summer among the wild flowers growing beside the sea wall and along the edges of creeks and banks you will find golden samphire, sea clover and the crimson-flowered grass vetchling.

5. After the lagoon the path leads over a grassy area kept more intensively grazed to provide breeding sites for lapwings, redshanks and skylarks. You may see the dark shapes of short-eared owls which hunt by day outlined against a winter sky and perhaps rarer predators such as hobbies or merlins.

Continue round the southernmost tip of the marshes past the old oyster beds and wide areas of saltmarsh to a gate close to the reserve's north-east corner.

6. Leave the Solent Way which continues through the gate and turn left down some steps and over a stile. Follow the path over the grass close to a fence on the left to a gate.

7. Past the gate, turn left down a track. When the track divides bear right towards the warden's hut. Benches inside provide a sheltered place to rest. Opposite the hut is grassland with free access. So go through the gate ahead to cross this fascinating area in the direction of the reserve entrance. The short turf is crossed by little winding creeks and dotted with ponds. Rabbits scuttle for cover under thickets of brambles and hawthorns. Among low-growing shrubs you will find the pink flowers of restharrow shaped like miniature sweet peas. In winter flocks of fieldfares and redwings arrive from Scandinavia to feast on hawthorn berries.

The sea wall at Farlington Marshes

From the reserve entrance retrace your steps along the sea wall and over Ports Creek to your car.

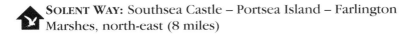 **SOLENT WAY:** Southsea Castle – Portsea Island – Farlington Marshes, north-east (8 miles)

Fine sea views can be enjoyed as the Way traces the southern shore of Portsea Island then heads north along a very pleasant coastal path beside Langstone Harbour before following the route of the pub walk around Farlington Marshes.

Southsea Castle is on your left as you follow the promenade along the sea front towards South Parade pier. Just beyond the pier and the canoe lake stand the remains of Lumps Fort. Ahead beyond Eastney Point is the western shore of Hayling Island and the narrow entrance to Langstone Harbour. Pass the Royal Marines Museum and follow the main road as it bears left over a road to the ferry to a T-junction. Turn left, keeping to the main road (Henderson Road) to pass Eastney Pumping Station built in 1887 and housing two beam engines.

A few yards past the pumping station turn right to follow a footpath over a park. Keep on down the road ahead and bear right in front of

St James' Hospital. When the road bends left, just past the Old Oyster House pub, keep straight on down a narrow footpath to the right of Langstone Harbour. On the right is the remaining section of a canal that once connected Arundel with Portsmouth. From the bridge you have a good view of a broken caisson, intended to form part of a Mulberry harbour, now stranded on Sinah sands.

Turn left along the harbourside footpath for around 3 miles joining the route of Walk 13 just before the bridge over Ports Creek (point 2). Follow the pub walk as far as the north-east corner of Farlington Marshes (end of point 5), then turn to Walk 14, page 94.

FACTFILE

Stagecoach Coastline run buses from Portsmouth Hard to Anchorage Park. Telephone: 01903 237661.

Hilsea Station is close to Anchorage Road. For rail times telephone: 08457 484950.

The Royal Marines Museum tells the story of the Royal Marines from 1664 to the present day with dramatic displays and audio-visual effects. Open daily, 10 am to 5.30 pm from Whitsun to August and 10 am to 4.30 pm from September to May. Telephone: 01705 819385.

WALK 14

HARBOUR LIGHTS –
LANGSTONE AND EMSWORTH

(Solent Way: Farlington Marshes, north-east –
Bedhampton – Langstone – Emsworth)

The Ship Inn

*The final section of the Solent Way is included in this circular walk.
We start from the quay at Langstone, a picturesque cluster of old
cottages and inns beside the channel linking Langstone and Chichester
Harbours. A path close to the northern shore of Chichester Harbour
leads us to the end of the Solent Way at Emsworth, once famous for its
oysters and tide mills now a busy yachting centre. Our return route
offers a few surprises! These include a walk along a 'twitten' and a
nostalgic look at the days of steam as we follow the track of the
former 'Hayling Billy' line.*

Langstone Quay was once busy with local barges unloading their cargoes, principally of Hampshire grain. Three mills were kept at full stretch supplying flour for the dockyard at Portsmouth, with demand increasing dramatically during the Napoleonic Wars. Overlooking the quay stands a vivid reminder of those times, the Ship Inn. During the 18th century the building was a wharfside warehouse handling grain and the original wheel hoist can still be seen in the roof of the Top Deck bar. Now the Ship is a pub to delight the hearts of all who love the sea. Come aboard to discover a treasure chest of all things nautical: model boats, old prints, nets and lobster pots, even a full size rowing boat.

As you might expect, the Ship is famous for its fresh fish which included when we called whole plaice and skate wings and a tempting 'Nibbles Platter' with mushrooms, onions, garlic bread and prawns. Other dishes included rack of ribs and Cajun chicken. Real ales are supplied by Gale's. On offer are Butser, GB and HSB and the award winning cask conditioned Festival Mild Ale. There is a well chosen wine list and Gale's also supply 21 old country wines.

Opening times on Monday to Saturday are 11 am to 11 pm, with food served from 12 noon to 2 pm and from 6.30 pm to 9.30 pm. On Sundays the pub is open from 12 noon to 10.30 pm and food is served from 12 noon to 9 pm.

From this quayside pub you enjoy a spendid view over Chichester Harbour to Hayling Island particularly from the windows of the Top Deck bar. And in summer the Ship offers a challenge to the more adventurous! A raft race takes place each year and anyone who can build a raft can enter. Phone the pub for details. Telephone: 02392 471719.

• HOW TO GET THERE: From the A27 Portsmouth–Chichester road turn south along the A3023, signed for Hayling Island. Continue for about ½ mile to the Ship on the left just before the bridge to Hayling Island.
• PARKING: On the quay, opposite the Ship.
• LENGTH OF THE WALK: 5 miles. Map: OS Explorer 120 Chichester (GR 718048).

THE WALK

1. Leave the front of the Ship Inn on your left and follow the foreshore past a watchtower and a row of coastguards' cottages, reminders of Langstone's smuggling days. An old brig, the *Griper*, was moored permanently offshore with a coastguard aboard but no smuggler was ever caught! As you come to the foot of Langstone High Street you will

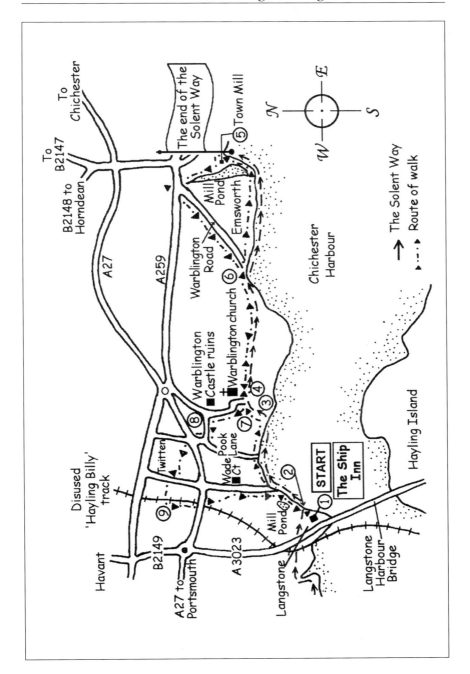

see the raised route of the old Wadeway crossing the harbour to Hayling Island, marked by posts. Now cut by a disused canal, it was once the only footway to the island.

2. On the corner of the High Street we join the Solent Way. Continue along the shore past the 18th century Royal Oak pub. The path curves right between a former tide mill and the mill pond. A windmill stands close by, converted into a dwelling house by the artist Flora Twort. Pass the quay at the foot of Pook Lane and continue to cross a stile.

3. Bear half-left diagonally over the field ahead to enter Warblington churchyard. At the first crosspath turn left. Take the third path on the right to the north-east corner, leave through a gate, cross a lane and follow the footpath ahead running to the right of Warblington church. This charming 12th and 13th century church once stood in the centre of a village, deserted after the Black Death. The two brick and flint huts in the corners of the churchyard were built for gravewatchers. The enormous yew tree is 1,500 years old!

4. Follow the path over fields and through woods to Emsworth waterfront. The village is built between two natural inlets dammed to power tide mills. Pass the most westerly mill and cross a lane to follow a sign leading to the sea wall built in 1760 to contain the western mill pond. The path follows the wall for over 200 yards as it curves round to meet the Town Mill on the other side of the inlet. On the quay beside the mill we come to the end of the Solent Way.

5. You might like to explore Emsworth, before turning left to follow Bridgefoot Path beside the westerly inlet to the A259. Turn left and after about 50 yards turn left again down Warblington Road to return to the foreshore.

6. Bear right and retrace your steps to Warblington church.

7. Do not enter the new churchyard but turn right up the lane leaving the church on your right. The lane doglegs left then right. The ruins of Warblington Castle are over the field on your right. Only the tower forming part of the gatehouse and an adjoining archway remain of the 16th century house built by the Countess of Salisbury. Her opposition to Henry VIII's divorce led to her execution on Tower Hill.

Town Mill, Emsworth, the end of the Solent Way

8. Take the first turning on the left, Pook Lane, and when you come to a T-junction turn right to cross the bridge over the A27. At the other side turn immediately left down a narrow path with a 'no-cycling' sign. This is a twitten, one of several ancient rights-of-way which once crossed open countryside linking the Saxon settlements of Warblington, Langstone, Bedhampton and Havant. Cross a road, turn right for a few yards, then left to follow the next twitten to the track of the former branch line that ran from Havant to Hayling, the 'Hayling Billy' line.

9. Bear left along the track which tunnels under the A27. Shortly after, look carefully for a small bridge over a stream on your left. Cross the bridge and walk over the field ahead to a lane. Turn right down the lane past Wade Court to return to the foreshore. Bear right to retrace your steps to the Ship.

SOLENT WAY: Farlington Marshes, north-east – Bedhampton – Langstone – Emsworth (6 miles)

Before joining the route of the pub walk at Langstone the Solent Way visits Bedhampton, passing The Old Mill House where John Keats wrote the final stanzas of his romantic poem 'The Eve of St Agnes'. The route also offers fine views of Langstone Harbour.

From the north-east corner of the marshes continue through a gate bearing right to follow the coast. Cross a car park and a public hard then bear left beside a creek. Cross the bridge over the A27 and follow the path towards a bridge over the railway, just south of Old Bedhampton. Just before the bridge turn right beside the railway. Over the fields on your right is the Old Mill House. Turn right in front of a brick wall and after a few yards bear left. The Hermitage Stream is on your right and your route shortly crosses it over an iron bridge. Immediately, look for two stiles on your right, cross, then walk diagonally south-east down the field ahead. Cross a road and follow the path as it bears left then up steps to take you over the bridge crossing the A27. Turn right and at the next road bear right for a few yards to cross to a footpath on the left running beside a stream. Cross the bridge to the other side to pass a large working wharf.

The path curves left round the shore and follows the sea wall skirting South Moor. Follow the wall as it bears left beside a creek. Pass a brick bridge and turn right over the next bridge. Continue along Mill Lane to

The path by the Mill at Langstone

meet the A3023. Cross and follow the road ahead, Langstone High Street, to join the route of the pub walk by the harbour (point 2). Continue to Town Mill in Emsworth and the end of the Solent Way.

FACTFILE

Stagecoach Coastline run buses from Portsmouth to Langstone Quay. Telephone: 01903 237661.

Warblington church, well worth a visit, is locked, but the key can be obtained from a cottage 100 yards up the road (see the church notice board).